Date Due

FRINGE BANKING

FRINGE BANKING

Check-Cashing Outlets, Pawnshops, and the Poor

John P. Caskey

RUSSELL SAGE FOUNDATION / NEW YORK

The Russell Sage Foundation

The Russell Sage Foundation, one of the oldest of America's general purpose foundations, was established in 1907 by Mrs. Margaret Olivia Sage for "the improvement of
social and living conditions in the United States." The Foundation seeks to fulfill this
mandate by fostering the development and dissemination of knowledge about the
country's political, social, and economic problems. While the Foundation endeavors
to assure the accuracy and objectivity of each book it publishes, the conclusions and
interpretations in Russell Sage Foundation publications are those of the authors and
not of the Foundation, its Trustees, or its staff. Publication by Russell Sage, therefore,
does not imply Foundation endorsement.

Library of Congress Cataloging-in-Publication Data

Caskey, John P.
    Fringe banking : check-cashing outlets, pawnshops, and the poor /
John P. Caskey.
        p.   cm.
    Includes bibliographical references and index.
    ISBN 0-87154-195-5
    1. Pawnbroking—United States.   2. Check cashing services—United
States.   3. Poor—United States—Finance, Personal.   I. Title.
HG2101.C37   1994
332.7'4—dc20   94-8244
                                                                CIP

Copyright © 1994 by Russell Sage Foundation. All rights reserved. Printed in the
United States of America. No part of this publication may be reproduced, stored in a
retrieval system, or transmitted, in any form or by any means, electronic, mechanical,
photocopying, recording, or otherwise, without the prior written permission of the
publisher.

The paper used in this publication meets the minimum requirements of American
National Standard for Information Sciences—Permanence of Paper for Printed Library
Materials, ANSI Z39.48-1992.

RUSSELL SAGE FOUNDATION
112 East 64th Street, New York, New York 10021

10 9 8 7 6 5 4 3 2 1

For Byran O. Jackson.
One of the kindest people I have known.
You will be sorely missed.

Contents

List of Tables
and Figures

Figures

Preface and
Acknowledgments

Many people have questioned the genesis of my interest in pawn-shops and check-cashing outlets, since my major professional focus has been on banks and monetary economics. Several years ago, my curiosity about pawnshops was piqued by hearing an interview with a pawnbroker on National Public Radio. Subsequently, an afternoon in the library revealed that no economist had analyzed the role of the pawnbroker in the financial system for over 30 years. I thought that I might undertake such a study, to investigate why and when pawnbroking had died out. When I discovered that it had not died out but, in fact, had boomed over the 1980s, I had to change the premise of my study. My investigation of pawnshops led naturally into a study of check-cashing outlets, which serve many of the same customers and which also had grown explosively over the 1980s.

Because pawnshops and check-cashing outlets have received little attention from academics, public policy analysts, and regulators of financial institutions, I had to use a variety of research methods in carrying out this project. I gathered quantitative data on fringe banks wherever that was possible; to check the reasonableness of the data and to address a number of issues not covered by the quantitative data, I interviewed pawnbrokers and check cashers across the country; I attended annual conventions of the National Pawnbrokers Association and the National Check Cashers Association; I interviewed numerous state regulators and spoke with an informal, unscientific sample of fringe banking customers.

In researching and writing this book, I have been helped by many institutions and individuals. First, I must express my gratitude to the Russell Sage Foundation for sponsoring much of the research that underlies this book. I am grateful for its financial support, and especially value the summer I spent in residence at the Foundation, exchanging ideas with the staff and other visiting scholars. I also thank Charlotte Shelby, Managing Editor at the Foundation, for her outstanding editorial contribution.

My 6-year visiting association with the Research Department at the Federal Reserve Bank of Kansas City has also been critically important in this project. I am particularly appreciative of the opportunity to test my ideas in the Bank's seminar series, to receive critical comments on drafts of papers written for its working paper series, and to publish some of my research in the Bank's journal. As the economists there well know, many of the ideas in this monograph were first tested on them over lunch.

Much of the research and writing for this book was completed at three institutions: Swarthmore College, Yale University, and the Universidad Nova de Lisboa. I am especially grateful for the support of my colleagues at Swarthmore and the valuable assistance of its skilled librarians. On a sabbatical from Swarthmore, I gained immensely from spending a year as a visiting faculty member in Yale's Department of Economics and a semester at the Universidad Nova in Lisbon, Portugal. The faculty and staff at both of these excellent universities were generous hosts.

Among the individuals who contributed to this project, I am most indebted to some first-rate Swarthmore College students who worked with me as co-authors of papers and as research assistants. In alphabetical order, they are Jennifer Ekert, Reade Kem, Andrew Peterson, Bart Yavorosky, and Brian Zikmund-Fisher. I am also grateful to numerous professional colleagues, especially Janet Ceglowski, Robinson Hollister, Hyman Minsky, and anonymous reviewers, who commented on earlier drafts of the manuscript and related articles. Special thanks go to Hyman

Minsky for helping me to arrive at the term "fringe banks" as a shorthand phrase covering both pawnshops and check-cashing outlets. I thank Catherine Mansell Carstens, F.J.A. Bouman, T.G. Ford, and Michael Skully for generously sharing their knowledge of pawnshop operations in other countries. I am indebted to Mike Hudson for informing me of the operations and rapid growth of rent-to-own stores. I thank Bill and Sara Caskey for editorial suggestions.

This book could not have been written without the cooperation of many pawnbrokers and commercial check cashers. Although I am sure that I omit some names, among the pawnbrokers who contributed the most are A.W. Eckert, Dick George, Angela and Israel Goltzman, Todd Gordon, Mark Leonard, John Marshall, Stan Meyerson, Gary Nopp, Dennis Preston, Jimmy and Louise Seawrite, and Mitch Wolf. Jim Keville and Jim Maguire of the Provident Loan Society offered helpful insights into the Society's unique operations. Jerry Stokes, the former publisher of *Today's Pawnbroker*, was always willing to share his perspective on the industry. Among the check cashers who were most helpful to my research, I note Robert Battini, Steve Bell, Robert Bortel, Robert Bucceri, Judith Fekete, Jerome Gagerman, Ray Hemmig, Michael Levitt, Ian MacKechnie, Howard Mandelbaum, Brett Polen, Eddie Rosario, and Ron Weinraub.

In conducting this research, I was also fortunate to encounter several people in state regulatory agencies who were especially helpful in providing data or sharing their knowledge: William Beatty (Pennsylvania), Steven Geary (Missouri), Doug Johnson (Florida), John McClure (Oklahoma), William McDonald (Connecticut), Sunny Phillips (Florida), Gail Smith (Oregon), Charles Wright (Indiana), and Myron Zaidman (New York). I thank you all.

Finally, it is with much love that I thank Janet Ginzberg for serving as a critical sounding board and for providing numerous editorial suggestions and steadfast moral support.

All the people and institutions named above contributed to the research or writing of the manuscript, but the ideas, opinions, and mistakes in the final product are mine alone. In fact, I'm quite confident that many of those named above would strongly disagree with some of what I have written.

Some sections of this book draw heavily on earlier articles by me and two co-authors previously published, or to be published, in the *Eastern Economic Journal* 20 (1) (Winter 1994); the Federal Reserve Bank of Kansas City *Economic Review* (March/April 1990 and November/December 1991); the *Journal of Money, Credit, and Banking* 23 (1) (February 1991) [Copyright 1991 Ohio State University Press. All rights reserved.]; and the *Urban Affairs Quarterly* 29 (4) (June 1994).

Why Study Fringe Banks?

The United States financial system is undergoing a transformation. Many of the changes—the erosion of regulatory barriers between banks and securities firms or the rise in interstate banking—have been widely noted and discussed. But one important development has crept in, almost completely unobserved—a rapid, nationwide expansion in the number of pawnshops and commercial check-cashing outlets. These so-called fringe banks provide credit and payment services primarily to low- and moderate-income households, many of which rarely interact with the formal banking system.

Despite the sparse attention that fringe banks receive, they are a significant part of the financial system, providing financial services to millions of households. In fact, although the popular notion is that pawnshops are a relic of the nineteenth century, pawnbroking has grown rapidly over the 1980s. There are more pawnshops today, both in absolute numbers and on a per capita basis, than at any time in United States history. Similarly, check-cashing outlets (CCOs), which charge a fee to cash customers' checks (mainly paychecks or government support checks), sell money orders, and make wire transfers, existed in only a handful of urban areas prior to the mid-1970s. Over the 1980s, however, the industry expanded rapidly, and now there are large numbers of CCOs in cities throughout the country.

In addition to its booming growth in the past decade, the fringe banking industry has become increasingly sophisticated as large national chains have replaced independently owned and operated stores. Pawnshops and CCOs have also spread beyond their traditional concentration in low-income urban areas into lower-middle-class suburban communities.

This rapid expansion in pawnshops and check-cashing outlets is particularly striking in view of their relatively high fees. Pawnshops commonly charge annualized interest rates of 200–250 percent for small, secured loans. And CCOs generally charge 1.5–2.5 percent of the face value of the customer's paycheck. A worker with an annual take-home pay of $12,000 can spend $250 a year just to convert his paychecks into cash. Given these comparatively high fees, fringe banks thrive by serving customers who are excluded from mainstream financial institutions and by differentiating their services from those of banks.[1] Pawnshops provide small, fast loans primarily to customers with bad credit histories, low incomes, high debt-to-income ratios, or unstable employment patterns—characteristics that exclude them from unsecured loans. Check-cashing outlets mainly serve customers who value their convenient locations, hours, and speed; who do not have bank accounts; or who have insufficient funds in their accounts to permit them to cash their paychecks.

This book is the first extended study of the roles that fringe banks play in the financial system. The motivations for the study are threefold. First, since pawnshops and check-cashing outlets are the primary financial institutions for millions of households, a knowledge of their operations is essential to a comprehensive understanding of the financial system. Second, fringe banks are a rapidly growing component of the financial system, which raises intriguing questions about the factors driving this growth. Third, pawnshops and CCOs deliver financial services primarily to low- and moderate-income households. Consequently, social concerns

---

[1]The term "bank" is generically used to include commercial banks, savings banks, and savings and loans. When it does not have this meaning, I explicitly indicate that it is to be understood in a more restricted sense.

about the economic situation and constraints facing these households make fringe banks a natural focus of study.

Because of my background in financial economics, this study of fringe banks emphasizes the economics of the institutions themselves, rather than that of their customers. Nevertheless, it is impossible to consider fringe banking without inquiring into consumer behavior and crossing numerous boundaries in academic disciplines. One is forced, for example, to address issues in financial economics, regulation and industrial organization, the economics of poverty, sociology, and psychology. This should be evident from the topics that are the primary focus of the study: explaining the services that pawnshops and check-cashing outlets provide and the fees they charge for these services; describing who uses pawnshops and check-cashing outlets and why they choose to do so; examining the factors responsible for the fringe banking boom of the 1980s; and investigating how fringe banks are, and should be, regulated.

In studying pawnshops and check-cashing outlets, this book does not address all of the issues relevant to the delivery of financial services to low- and moderate-income households. For lack of data, it does not examine financial services in the informal sector, such as check cashing by bars or lending by unlicensed individuals. And since its primary focus is on consumer payment services and credit, it does not discuss community development loan funds, which lend primarily for low-income housing development; nor community development banks, such as the South Shore Bank in Chicago; nor micro-loan funds, which lend for very small business projects. Nor does it investigate whether banks discriminate on racial grounds in home mortgage lending.[2]

Finally, it is worth noting that the Russell Sage Foundation, in sponsoring much of the research that served as the basis for this book, has returned to issues in which it was involved in its early years, thereby creating some interesting historical parallels. The Foundation was created in 1907 by Russell Sage's widow, Margaret Olivia Sage. Russell Sage had been an extraordinarily successful financier who controlled numerous major corporations, including the Western Union Company, which today provides

[2]Major studies on this topic are referenced by James T. Campen (1993).

money-wiring services to check-cashing outlets and which has recently begun to build its own chain of CCOs. One of Mrs. Sage's principal advisors in creating the Foundation was Robert W. de Forest, who in 1894 helped found New York City's public interest pawnshop, the Provident Loan Society. Mr. de Forest convinced Mrs. Sage to make consumers' small-loan problems a primary focus of the Foundation. Accordingly, in 1909 the Foundation began to promote the creation of low-cost consumer loan funds, which were to be capitalized by wealthy individuals who ". . . recognized that under modern conditions of life many persons who had no banking facilities needed at times small temporary loans" (Glenn et al. 1947, p. 136).

In 1910 the Foundation created a division to study abuses by financial institutions serving low- and moderate-income households and to advocate legislative reforms to curb such activities. Over the next decade, the division published studies of the salary and chattel loan businesses, fought to limit the activities of illegal moneylenders, and drafted model small-loan legislation. In 1922 the Foundation commissioned a former Swarthmore College economics professor, Louis Robinson, to direct a comprehensive study of the regulated small loan business. This project resulted in the publication of *The Regulation of Pawnbroking* (R. Cornelius Raby 1924) and *Ten Thousand Small Loans* (Louis Robinson and Maude E. Sterns 1930). In the decade that followed, the Foundation continued to sponsor research in the field and published several more pioneering studies of consumer credit markets. In the 1940s, however, the Foundation abandoned the study of low-income consumer financial markets as it focused its efforts in other areas. In sponsoring this research more than 50 years later, the Foundation has returned to its roots.

1 / Four Themes

The following chapters investigate in depth how pawnshops and CCOs function, who uses these institutions, and for what reasons. They also discuss the factors behind the recent rapid growth in fringe banking and examine the case for regulating pawnshops and CCOs. This initial chapter, however, steps back from the details and sets out the four major themes that emerge in the book.

The first theme is that households without financial savings must often pay more than other households for basic financial services. This observation includes financial markets in a pattern that has long been recognized in markets for nonfinancial goods and services (see Caplovitz 1963). For example, people living in areas with high concentrations of low-income households must often patronize a small number of local retail outlets that charge more for their products and offer a more limited selection of products than do retail stores in middle- and upper-income areas (Andreasen 1975). Stores in low-income urban areas that sell consumer durables commonly offer less favorable credit terms or market their products through rental-purchase agreements that greatly increase the effective price of the goods. While there is little disagreement that retail prices are higher in low-income urban areas, there is much disagreement over why this is so. Community activists often charge that the retailers in low-income areas use local monopoly power to exploit their customers. The retailers respond that their costs are significantly higher than those of retailers in more affluent areas.

Financial markets are no exception to the rule that the poor pay more. But the relevant measure of poverty in financial markets is not household income; rather, it is the household's ability to maintain financial savings.[1] Although these two measures are closely related, they are not perfectly correlated. A family's ability to maintain savings depends on its income level as well as its structure, stability of income, special needs, and lifestyle choices.

Families that do not maintain financial savings often have bad credit records or debt to income ratios that exclude them from mainstream sources of consumer credit. This is true for several reasons. Such families have no financial margin of safety; even temporary disruptions in family earnings or unforeseen expenditure needs can interfere with their ability to service outstanding debts. Families without financial savings are often headed by individuals with low incomes and low education levels who may experience periods of unemployment and drastic earnings fluctuations. Other families cannot maintain savings because of expensive special needs, such as major medical bills, and may be forced to accumulate substantial debts. Paying for necessary medical care can understandably claim a higher priority than servicing accumulated debts. Finally, households that do not maintain savings because of lifestyles that are expensive relative to their incomes are likely to be near the limit of their debt service capacity and may not have had the financial discipline or foresight to meet past debt service obligations.

In addition to being cut off from major consumer credit sources, households without financial savings are often excluded from mainstream payment services. One must maintain a deposit account at a bank or similar institution to write a check. Similarly, banks generally cash checks drawn on other banks only for their

---

[1]In another context, Michael Sherraden (1991) discusses this distinction in detail in *Assets and the Poor: A New American Welfare Policy.*

own depositors. Even those with deposit accounts must commonly wait for a check to clear through the banking system before withdrawing the cash if they do not maintain a sufficient balance in their account to cover the check.

Since households without financial savings are often excluded from the credit and payment services of mainstream financial institutions, many must turn to pawnshops and CCOs to meet these needs. Fringe banks, however, are a costly alternative. Pawnshop credit is commonly ten to fifteen times more expensive than consumer loans from banks. The payment services of CCOs are four to six times as expensive as those of banks. Although local monopoly power may account for a part of these fees, this is not the major factor. Rather, fringe banking fees are high because the cost of providing the credit or payment service is high relative to the size of the transaction.

The second theme that emerges in this study is that the 1980s boom in fringe banking and the increasing segmentation of consumer financial markets reflected the increasing polarization in the economic well-being of American families. The incomes of millions of households at the lower end of the income distribution fell or stagnated. Combined with other socioeconomic changes, the percentage of the population living from one paycheck to the next with no financial savings of note increased over the 1980s. Since bank payment services are largely restricted to bank depositors, people without financial savings had to turn elsewhere for basic payment services. Similarly, the falling standards of living of many lower-income households meant that more of them were cut off from mainstream credit sources, forcing them to turn to pawnshops to meet credit needs.

Changes in banking regulations and bank policies, which indirectly reflected changes in ideology, technology, and the inflation of the 1970s, also contributed to the fringe banking boom.[2] Toward

---

[2]In economic history there are numerous examples to reinforce the notion that changes in social conditions, technology, ideology, and macroeconomic conditions shape financial systems. The development of bond and stock markets in the first half of the nineteenth century was closely related to the technological advances that led to the steam engine, large factories, railroads, and the telegraph (Krooss and Blyn 1971). In the late nineteenth century, the rise of huge business trusts and industrial giants with massive financial needs increased the importance of Wall Street and led to the creation of chains of retail brokerage houses to sell stock and bond instruments to

the end of the 1970s, economists, policymakers, and the public became much more critical of regulation, viewing it as largely serving special economic interests. At the same time, historically high inflation and accompanying high interest rates placed banks at a competitive disadvantage to securities markets, since legal ceilings existed for interest rates on bank deposits but not for interest rates on commercial paper or bonds. The diffusion of low-cost computer technology played a vital role in the development of money market mutual funds and interstate banking by "nonbank" banks, accentuating the competitive disadvantage of traditional banks. These developments led the government to lift controls on bank deposit interest rates and to promote competition in consumer financial markets (Litan 1987). The resulting increase in competitive pressures forced banks to pay higher interest rates to attract large deposits and to eliminate some money-losing services that they had previously cross-subsidized, such as the provision of low-cost, small-balance deposit accounts. The increased cost of small-balance deposit accounts encouraged many households with limited financial savings to abandon the banking system. And, in response to competitive pressures, banks closed unprofitable or marginally profitable branches, many of which were in low-income areas. These developments combined to spur the demand for fringe banking services.

The third theme of this study is that, although many households patronize fringe banks because they have no practical alternatives, a significant share of pawnshop and CCO customers use these institutions on a discretionary basis. It is not unusual, for example, for a pawnshop customer to borrow to pay for a vacation, an evening's entertainment, or other discretionary expenditures. Many people using check-cashing outlets could wait 3 to 5 days for their checks to clear through a bank, but they prefer to pay a fee to get the cash immediately, or they value the convenient

---

the public across the country. In the early twentieth century, the mass marketing of the automobile and other consumer durables to the growing middle class led to rapid growth in casualty insurance and consumer finance companies. The Depression and associated congressional hearings led the public to demand greater safety and stability in the financial system, especially for financial institutions or markets used by the middle class. This resulted in new laws that radically restructured the financial system by separating commercial banking from investment banking, creating the Securities and Exchange Commission, and insuring deposit accounts in banks.

location and operating hours of a CCO. In other words, some people turn to fringe banks out of necessity, but others do so because they believe that the services these institutions provide are worth the fees.

Critics argue that many of the low- and moderate-income households who patronize fringe banks on a discretionary basis exhibit poor judgment; that these households either base their decisions on incorrect information about the relative convenience and cost of fringe banks or that they demonstrate an irrationally short time horizon in budgeting expenditures. Such critics claim that many people patronizing fringe banks on a discretionary basis are wasting their money without regard to the longer term consequences. These criticisms of the economic behavior of lower-income families can be socially divisive and controversial, but any comprehensive analysis of fringe banking must acknowledge them. If the discretionary use of fringe banks arises from mistakes in judgment, an increased emphasis on consumer education would be an appropriate response to the problem.

The fourth and final theme that emerges from this study is that insufficient resources are devoted to regulating and monitoring fringe banking markets. Our society devotes substantial resources to protecting consumers in the financial markets and institutions serving middle- and upper-income households. These measures are justified by a number of considerations. Bank depositors, for example, cannot obtain the information that they would need to evaluate the riskiness of a bank's loan portfolio. Even if the information were available, most depositors would not know how to use it. In addition, it can be more cost-effective to have a regulator set limits on bank risk-taking and insure deposits rather than rely on market mechanisms to limit bank risk-taking. In securities markets, where it is assumed that more sophisticated investors interact, regulations insist on disclosure of relevant information and the prevention of insider trading.[3]

In the case of fringe banking, there are similar justifications for

[3] The stability of banks and securities markets is linked to aggregate economic stability. These institutions and markets are also critically important in allocating savings to productive investment projects. In addition to consumer protection issues, these considerations are used to justify many of the regulations governing banks and securities markets.

regulation. The vast majority of customers are far less sophisticated in economics than are the owners or managers of fringe banks. In fact, many customers would have difficulty converting a fee, stated in percentage terms, into a dollar figure. As in mainstream financial markets, customers also cannot obtain information that should be relevant to their decision to patronize a particular fringe bank. Pawnshop customers, for example, must leave their collateral with a broker without knowing how well the broker cares for the collateral or what steps the broker takes to protect against losses from fire or theft.

Despite these similarities to mainstream financial markets, very few resources are devoted to regulating fringe banks. The federal government does not specifically monitor or regulate pawnshops or CCOs. Most states do regulate pawnshops. The vast majority, however, do not collect any data on the industry and devote almost no resources to enforcing the regulations. A minority of states regulate commercial check-cashing outlets. Of those that do, even fewer monitor practices in the industry or devote meaningful resources to enforcing the regulations. Undoubtedly, much of the disparity between the resources devoted to consumer protection in mainstream financial markets and those devoted to regulating and monitoring fringe banks is explained by differences in the economic and political power of their customers. In a just system, however, the recognition that most pawnshop and CCO customers have little economic or political power should increase the priority of consumer protection measures in these markets.

The subsequent seven chapters present the data and analyses behind these four themes. To place recent developments in an historical context, Chapter 2 discusses the evolution of pawnbroking and commercial check cashing in the United States from the colonial period through the early 1970s. Chapter 3 examines the operations of contemporary pawnshops and CCOs and documents the rapid growth in fringe banking over the 1980s. Chapter 4 describes who uses pawnshops and check-cashing outlets and why they choose to do so. Chapter 5 studies the factors responsible for the 1980s boom in fringe banking. Chapter 6 explains why pawnshop and check-cashing fees are high compared to fees for similar services from mainstream financial institutions and examines the case for regulating fringe banks. Chapter 7 briefly reviews public policy proposals aimed at improving the access of lower-income households to mainstream deposit institutions. The final chapter speculates on future growth prospects for pawnshops and check-cashing outlets and discusses some of the broader economic and social policy implications raised by the increased segmentation of consumer financial markets.

2 / A Brief History of Pawnbroking and Commercial Check Cashing

A pawnshop loan is a relatively simple transaction: the broker makes a fixed term loan to a consumer who leaves collateral in the possession of the broker. If the customer repays the loan and all required fees, the broker returns the collateral to the customer. If the customer does not repay the loan by a specified date, the collateral becomes the property of the broker and the customer's debt is extinguished. Because pawnshop loans are simple transactions, pawnshops are ancient financial institutions with a rich cultural and economic history.

Check-cashing outlets also provide a simple service. A customer endorses a third party's check payable to the customer (generally the customer's paycheck or government benefit check) and presents this check to the CCO in exchange for cash. The CCO pays less than the full face value of the check; the discount is the CCO's fee for the check-cashing service. Although there are historical antecedents to this business, commercial check cashing could not exist before bank checks became a common means to pay workers or to deliver government benefits. CCOs are therefore relatively new financial institutions; the first came into existence in the 1930s.

An examination of the historical evolution of pawnbroking and commercial check cashing indicates that the 1980s boom in fringe banking stands in sharp contrast to an earlier decline in pawnbroking and stagnation in the check-cashing industry. But there are many parallels between contemporary fringe banking and its antecedents. Under earlier institutional arrangements, for example, banks and other actors in the financial system commonly discounted checks and even currency. And although the items that people pawn have changed considerably over time, the basic operation of pawnshops and the reasons for their use have remained remarkably constant. The perceived problems addressed by contemporary laws regulating pawnbroking are also not new: governments have regulated pawnshops almost since their inception.

THE EVOLUTION OF PAWNBROKING

Informal pawnbroking has existed since ancient times. There are many Old Testament biblical references to loans based on pledges of personal property (Levine 1911, pp. 11–15). The earliest formal pawnshops, however, may have developed in China (Whelan 1979).[1]

In Europe, the earliest formal pawnshops appear to have been founded by the Franciscans of the Catholic Church toward the end of the fifteenth century (Kuznets 1933, pp. 34–35). These were not-for-profit pawnshops, known as *monti di pieta* in Italian or, roughly translated, "banks that take pity." The Franciscans opened them as a way to combat usury. The *monti di pieta* provided low-cost small collateralized loans to artisans and the poor.[2] In the next two centuries, the Church, municipal governments, and independent charitable groups opened similar philanthropic pawnshops in the major urban centers of Western and Central

---

[1] Today, pawnshops are well represented throughout Asia. In most countries, they are privately owned; government-owned pawnshops are, however, important in Thailand. F. J. A. Bauman and R. Houtman (1988) describe the functioning of pawnshops in Sri Lanka. Mario Lamberte (1988) studied their role in the financial system of the Philippines. Michael Skully (1992) provides an overview of pawnshop operations in several Asian countries.

[2] At least one major contemporary Italian commercial bank, Il Monte dei Paschi di Siena, evolved from one of these early pawnshops (Green 1991).

Europe.[3] As the Church lost influence, more and more of these
were operated by municipal governments. The municipal pawnshops sought to charge low interest rates on loans and return any
surplus on forfeited pledges to the customer; the surplus being
the difference between the amount earned from the sale of the
collateral and the amount the customer would have to pay to
redeem the collateral.

Where the law did not outlaw them, private pawnbrokers also
existed in Europe. Although they charged higher interest rates
than did the municipal pawnshops, they were used by some borrowers because they made larger loans on collateral, were more
discreet, or more conveniently located. In England, not-for-profit
pawnshops never took root, and private pawnshops were the
rule. Their operations were, however, regulated by the government. Although very early records are incomplete, the first statutory regulation of British pawnshops was apparently imposed in
1603 (Levine 1911, p. 35). In 1784–1785, the British government
established national licensing requirements and set ceilings on
pawnshop interest rates (Kuznets 1933; see also Hudson 1982 and
Tebbutt 1983).

British pawnshops were apparently the first to use the three
balls as a symbol for the profession. The most compelling explanation of the symbol is that it originated in the mid-eighteenth century in Britain, when

> . . . the three balls, either golden or blue, became generally
> adopted by pawnbrokers as a sign of their trade. Before then,
> pawnbroking establishments were distinguished by a variety of
> signs, although the "Three Blue Balls" or "Three Blue Bowls"
> were much the most frequent. Blue was, in fact, a more fitting
> colour than gold, since the sign almost certainly comes from the
> three blue discs which appear on the lower part of the coat of
> arms of the Medicis, from whose territory the Lombard gold-

[3] Among the most famous still operating today are the Dorotheum in Vienna, which
was founded in 1707, and the *Crédit Municipal* in Paris, which was founded as a
mont-de-piété in 1777 (Dornberg 1990, Kuznets 1933). Marec (1983) provides an excellent
history of the *mont-de-piété* in Rouen from 1778 to 1982. Municipal pawnshops are also
important in Mexico. As of 1990, the main government-owned pawnshop in Mexico
had 30 branches and served about 4 million people annually.

smiths [the first great moneylenders in Britain] originally came. [Hudson 1982, p. 35]

Samuel Levine (1911, pp. 32–33), drawing on Hardaker (1892, p. 8), provides a similar account, adding that

> . . . the signs suspended over the doors of the Lombards were originally three flat yellow effigies of byzants, or gold coins, laid heraldically upon a field sable. But [pawnbrokers found it] . . . more convenient to convert the flat discs into spherical gilt balls, as glittering in the light they could be seen from all sides and so attract customers to the houses above which they were suspended.[4]

Pawnshops have played a role in American history since the colonization of the continent by Europeans. In fact, a pawnbroker is popularly credited with indirectly financing Columbus's discovery voyage to the Americas. According to legend, after rejecting Columbus's initial proposal that she finance his explorations, Isabella of Castile nobly pledged her jewels to raise money for the venture. Alfred Hardaker (1892, p. 15) relates that one nineteenth century author facetiously remarked, "If Americans had duly reflected on this incident . . . they certainly, with the stars and stripes had quartered the three balls in their national flag." Although colorful, the story of Isabella pawning her jewels to raise money for the explorations is apparently historically inaccurate (Sale 1990, p. 135).

---

[4]There is also a fanciful account that relates the three ball emblem to a legend involving St. Nicholas, the Bishop of Pantheria (Hardaker 1892, pp. 6–8; De Roover 1946). According to the legend, there was a poor starving nobleman in the town with three daughters. He was so poor that there appeared there would be no means of obtaining food for his daughters other than to sacrifice them to an "infamous" life. The maidens wept constantly from hunger and fear for their prospects. St. Nicholas, upon learning of this, contrived to provide for the man and his family. Accordingly, he wrapped three handfuls of gold in handkerchiefs, one for each daughter, and threw them in an open window of the poor man's house so the man would not know their origin. It is said that some early pawnbrokers, who saw themselves as helping those in financial distress, adopted the three gold balls to represent the three purses of gold in this legend.

A less benign interpretation of the three-ball symbol is provided by a traditional joke among pawnshop customers, which maintains that it means the odds are two to one that customers will never see their collateral again.

It is clear, however, that pawnbroking in the United States began before independence. Pawnbrokers were operating in New York City as early as 1657 and in Philadelphia by 1782 (Foulke 1941, pp. 114–115). These early pawnbrokers were generally second-hand goods dealers, often of used clothing, who drifted into the moneylending business. American pawnbroking followed the British model, where pawnshops were regulated profit-oriented businesses, rather than the nonprofit municipal organizations of Continental Europe.

By the early nineteenth century pawnbroking was well established in several major northeastern urban centers in the United States. In fact, in 1809, the Common Council of New York City received a petition from citizens complaining of ". . . the great number of Pawnbrokers and the unrestrained manner in which they conduct themselves" (Foulke 1941, p. 116). Pawnbroking was also active in Philadelphia and Boston in the 1820s (Foulke 1941, pp. 118–119).

It continued to grow over the nineteenth century and, by the end of the century, pawnshops were common in most urban areas throughout the country. Levine (1913, p. 30), using data collected from over 100 cities, estimated that in 1911 there were 1,976 licensed pawnbrokers in the country, or about one for every 47,500 inhabitants. He also noted that pawnshops were heavily concentrated in the major cities. To illustrate his point, he counted 201 pawnshops in Greater New York City, 102 in Philadelphia, 77 in Chicago, 72 in Boston, and 47 in San Francisco, 35 in Portland, 30 in Omaha, and 25 in New Orleans.

William Patterson, who wrote a Ph.D. dissertation on pawnbroking in 1898, explained the concentration of pawnshops in these urban areas with the observation that

> The business of the pawnbroker requires not only an urban population, but a dense urban population, such as is found in the great centers of industry. . . . [O]utside of the North Atlantic Section there are but few States with even two cities of sufficient size to support the business. [Patterson 1899, p. 256]

Patterson's point was that the average pawnshop loan was quite small, and pawnshops had to make a high volume of loans to be profitable. Outside of the major cities, they simply could not draw enough customers to survive because high personal transportation costs prevented people from traveling more than a short distance.[5]

As pawnbroking grew over the nineteenth century, the type of items people pledged for their loans changed. Pawnbrokers' records in New York City from 1828 are reported to have shown that 149,890 articles were pawned by 71,576 persons.[6] More than half of these pledges were of articles of clothing. Slightly less than one quarter of the pledges were of watches, table silver, rings, and jewelry. The records of one fairly typical New York City pawnshop, Simpson's, indicate the type of items pledged in 1835. On April 1, 1835, this pawnshop made 116 loans with a mean value of $1.93 (Simpson et al. 1954, pp. 28–29). Among the items pledged that day and the loans made on them were:

six linen sheets	$ 4.50
one vest	$ .25
four books	$ .38
one hat in box	$ .25
gold watch and chain	$12.00
one jacket and pair of boots	$ .50

By the end of the nineteenth century, it was becoming less common for pawnshops to accept common clothing as collateral. The mass production of clothing had cheapened its value and caused fashions to change rapidly, resulting in losses for brokers who could not sell the clothes quickly. This shift is indicated in pawnshop studies of the turn of the century. For example, in his Ph.D. dissertation, Patterson (1898, pp. 164–166) reported that in Minneapolis in 1892 about 58 percent of the pledges were watches and 80 percent were jewelry of some sort. Clothing and household goods were only 14 percent. Patterson stated that the average loan of the time was between $3 and $6.

Pawnbrokers did not ask their customers why they needed loans, since the loans were based only on the value of the collat-

---

[5] As the automobile and paved roads became common in the twentieth century, transportation costs fell dramatically and pawnshops began to appear in cities with populations as small as 10,000 and in less densely populated sections of large cities.

[6] Matthew Carey, *Public Charities of Philadelphia*. In miscellaneous *Essays*, printed for Carey and Hart, Philadelphia (1830, p. 160) as cited in Foulke (1941, p. 118).

eral. Nevertheless, many customers volunteered this information, and brokers drew their own inferences from observing their customers' behavior. After interviewing pawnbrokers across the country around 1910, Levine reported that

> Money is needed to meet such unexpected demands as aiding a relative, expenses of illness, costs of funerals. The slightest disturbance in the balance between the income and the outlay of a wage-earning individual . . . necessitates a "call" upon the pawnbroker. . . . Among pawnors are also to be found many whose incomes should be sufficient for their needs, but whose desires for maintaining a false social position oblige them temporarily to replenish their purses. [Levine 1913, pp. 5–6]

For many urban working-class people in nineteenth and early twentieth centuries, going to the pawnshop was almost a weekly routine. This was reflected in contemporary estimates of the scale of pawnshop operations. Writing in 1898, Patterson (p. 167) reported that ". . . the pawnbrokers of Philadelphia receive about 1,196,736 pawns per calendar year, or roughly one pledge per inhabitant."

The role of pawnshops in the daily lives of urban workers was also reflected in the language and culture of the time.[7] For example, rather than say that they were going to the pawnbroker, people would speak of going to see "uncle." One pawnbroker explained the possible origin of this expression:

> By 1826 the hock shop [Simpson's in New York City] was doing such a thriving business that the founder sent to England for two of his nephews . . . to work with him as apprentices. . . . These Simpson nephews . . . were responsible for the word "uncle" becoming a slang synonym of pawnbroker. When offered unfamiliar collateral during their years as apprentices, they would tell the customer, "I'll have to ask my uncle." [Simpson et al. 1954, p. 27]

While amusing, this account is probably inaccurate. The Oxford English Dictionary claims that the term "uncle" was used for

---

[7]In the post–World War II era, pawnshops continued to have a role in popular culture. The best known example may be the film, "The Pawnbroker," which was based on a novel with the same title. Songs, such as "Pittsburgh, Pennsylvania" and "Saturday Night Special," have also focused on pawnshops.

pawnbrokers in England as early as 1756. In French, the slang for a pawnshop is *ma tante* or *le clou,* which translate as "my aunt" or "the nail." The latter term is similar to our expression, "hock," which in nineteenth century English was the word for a chain with a hook at the end. At that time, in both France and England pawned items were commonly hung from hooks and nails on the walls, which explains the origin of these terms.

Pawnshops were also common in the novels of the nineteenth century social realists, such as Charles Dickens and Honoré de Balzac, and were referred to in more popular culture, such as the nursery rhyme "Pop Goes the Weasel" (Schwed 1975, pp. 210–211). The rhyme is attributed to the Englishman, W. R. Mondale, who composed it circa 1853. At that time, "pop" was a term meaning to pawn and "weasel" was the slang term for a flatiron used to press clothing. Two of the original verses of the nursery rhyme were:

A penny for a spool of thread
A penny for a needle,
That's the way the money goes—
Pop goes the weasel!

Potatoes for an Irishman's taste
The doctor for the measles,
That's the way the money goes—
Pop goes the weasel!

As pawnbroking flourished in the nineteenth century, civic-spirited citizens often denounced the industry as one that exploited the poor and facilitated the marketing of stolen goods. In fact, the *First Annual Report of the Society for the Prevention of Pauperism in the City of New York* (1818), included pawnbroking in its list of the causes of pauperism. The general attitude of the time among those concerned with the well-being of lower-income groups was expressed in a letter to a Philadelphia newspaper:

I wish . . . to call attention of the public to the alarming increase of Pawnbrokers. . . . These shops are little better than a common nuisance, and in the opinion of many respectable persons, are calculated to injure society by their demoralizing influence. . . . It is evident these institutions affect the poorer class of society

most, many of whom in time of sickness, death, and other af-
flictions in their families, take their goods to the pawnbrokers,
hoping in a short time to be able to redeem them again; but
scarcely one out of twenty ever becomes able. Although there
is a law to regulate the percentage of these money lenders, we
believe it is scarcely or ever put in force. [*Mechanics' Free Press*
June 28, 1828][8]

There were rebuttals to these views. Writing much later, Levine
argued:

It is absurd to charge the pawnbroker with being the cause of
the economic distress among the masses. . . . Not the pawnbroker, but those who have accumulated their riches regardless of
the effects of their activities upon the health and life of the
independent industrial class to which the pawnors belong, are
to blame for the resulting evils. [Levine 1913, p. 6]

Concerns that pawnbrokers exploited their customers and
traded in stolen goods led many municipalities and some states
to regulate the industry. These regulations typically required
pawnshops to be licensed and to provide local police with lists
of pledged collateral. The regulations commonly set interest rate
ceilings and specified the conditions under which the broker could
sell the collateral. For example, in 1812, the Common Council of
New York City passed an ordinance limiting pawnbrokers to a 25
percent annual interest rate on loans for $25 or less, and a 7 per-
cent annual interest rate on larger loans. The broker could sell the
collateral at a public auction after it had been in his possession
for one year, provided a notice was published in an authorized
newspaper giving the time and place of the sale. As indicated in
a *Harper's New Monthly Magazine* article of 1869, there was great
diversity across cities in the usury laws governing pawnshops:

. . . while Albany . . . lets the pawnbrokers pretty severely
alone, Buffalo allows . . . the collection of 3 percent per month,
with a forfeiture at one year. Rochester restricts the interest to
20 percent per annum, but allows a forfeiture at the end of six
months. Baltimore . . . fixes the interest at 6 percent per annum,

---

[8]I am grateful to Lori Ginzberg for bringing this letter to my attention.

but forces a renewal of the pawn ticket every month, and the payment of a "ticket fee" of 6 1/4 cents for each ticket under $3; of 9 cents for $5 and under, and so on up . . . with a forfeiture and sale at the end of six months, the surplus, "if any," to be held for the owner. Philadelphia somewhat resembles Baltimore in various respects, and allows 3 percent additional on sums of one dollar, with forfeiture at the end of one year. [Foulke 1941, pp. 160–161]

In some cases, the regulations were sufficiently burdensome to cause licensed pawnbrokers to stop operating within the city limits. In 1842, for example, when some Philadelphia citizens proposed starting a philanthropic pawnshop along the lines of those in Continental Europe, the city council replied that

. . . at present there is not a single pawnbroker doing business within the city limits. There [sic] absence may be accounted for by the tax of $50 imposed upon each one for a license to exercise that calling for one year. [Patterson 1898, pp. 171–172]

In the second half of the nineteenth century, an increasing number of states assumed responsibility for regulating pawnshops. By 1898 more than 30 had laws covering pawnshop operations. Some of these state laws however simply delegated the task to municipalities. By 1910, 14 states had laws requiring pawnbrokers to return to the customer any surplus from the sale of the collateral. Seventeen states set maximum interest rates on pawnshop loans. New Mexico permitted brokers to charge 10 percent interest a month; Delaware permitted 8 percent a month; and Arizona 4 percent. Several of the states permitted limited additional charges.[9] Other states with ceilings limited brokers to charging 3 percent a month or less. Rhode Island's statute prohibited the pawnbroker from lending to someone who

---

[9]In the 1920s, as part of its effort to improve and make more uniform state laws governing the consumer finance industry, the Russell Sage Foundation endorsed a model set of state pawnshop regulations, drafted by Cornelius Raby (1924). The model regulations called for a 3 percent monthly interest rate with a 15 cent minimum charge on loans. Any surplus was to be returned to the pledger. Although the model legislation was endorsed and published by the Foundation, it appears that no one devoted much effort to promoting it before state legislatures, and only a few states in the Northeast adopted versions of the bill.

. . . habitually spends his time in frequenting houses of ill fame, gaming houses, or that from drinking, idleness, or debauchery of any kind, he is squandering his earnings, or wasting his estate, or that he is likely to bring himself or his family to want, or to render himself or family a public charge. [Levine 1911, p. 70]

By the end of the nineteenth century, pawnshops were commonly regulated at the state or municipal level, but the regulations were rarely strictly enforced. In the 1850s, a committee in Boston examined that city's pawnbroking situation and concluded:

So far as we can judge, the rate of interest demanded and paid on loans is burdensome to the last degree, being ten to one hundred times the legal rate; one dollar a week on a loan of ten dollars not being an unusual charge. . . . In many offices we are told they [pawnbrokers] never give tickets in acknowledgement of the pledge, thus leaving the party pledging entirely at the broker's mercy. Stories of suffering and of wrong resulting from this mode of borrowing could be multiplied without number. [Patterson 1898, pp. 173–174]

Patterson (1898, pp. 160–161) reported that, 50 years later, many cities ". . . so loosely enforce their ordinance that the least ingenious pawnbroker is left perfectly free to follow his own desires." Moreover, some major cities ". . . after fixing the legal rate of interest, fail to limit or prohibit [other] charges, and so give the pawnbroker 'leave and license' to charge whatever rate he wishes. . . . In Philadelphia where the rate of charges is fixed at 2 percent per month, and interest at 6 percent per annum, making the greatest possible legal charge 2.5 percent per month, the brokers charge from 5.5 to 6 percent per month." In 1898, Philadelphia required that sales of forfeited pledges be by auction and that any surplus after the loan, interest, and charges were paid be returned to the owner. However, Patterson reported that ". . . the ordinance is not enforced, the brokers admitting that they allow only such pawns as they cannot sell at private sale to come to auction, and smile at the idea of returning the surplus to the owner." In another example: "Chicago appears very conservative with a rate of 36 percent per annum and no charges, but we understand the proviso is violated and 10 percent per month or 120 percent is the usual charge."

PHILANTHROPIC PAWNSHOPS

While many civic-minded citizens of the nineteenth and early twentieth century advocated stricter regulations for pawnshops, others argued that the public would be better served if municipalities or private philanthropies started their own pawnshops operated along the lines of the *mont-de-piété*. For example, the Boston committee that examined pawnshop operations in that city in the 1850s argued that countries in Continental Europe

> . . . recognize the fact not yet understood and appreciated here or in England, that the poor need, and must and will have loans at certain times. . . . The advantages of such an institution (*mont-de-piété*) over our pawnbroker system no one can fail for a moment to appreciate. In the first place, it is bound by law to loan on anything and everything of value offered, and at a rate reasonable and fixed. There is . . . no risk, no extortion, but everything safe, fixed, and above board. The poor of Paris get their loans at one tenth part of the price paid here. Is not the Continental mode eminently charitable, praiseworthy, and just? [Patterson 1898, pp. 175–176]

This report convinced several citizens in Boston to found in 1859 the Collateral Loan Company (CLC), which was to operate as a philanthropic pawnshop along the lines of the Paris *mont-de-piété*. The CLC had seven directors, five chosen by the shareholders, one appointed by the governor of the Commonwealth, and one by the mayor of Boston. Its initial interest rate on loans was 1.5 percent a month (raised to 2 percent in 1869), and loans were for a term of 1 year. Forfeited collateral was sold at public auction and any surplus was returned to the customer on demand. The CLC raised capital by selling shares paying limited dividends. Any profits after the dividends were paid were to be donated to charity, although later this rule was revised to allow some profits to be retained in order to build the CLC's capital. In 1896 its paid-up capital was $196,000. In 1893 its average loan was almost $13, more than twice that of most private pawnshops.

Following the opening of the Collateral Loan Company, similar philanthropic pawnshops opened in several other cities. The most notable of these was the Provident Loan Society (PLS) in New York City. It was founded in 1894 by a group of prominent financiers, including George Baker, Solomon Loeb, J. Pierpont Morgan, Percy Rockefeller, Jacob and Mortimer Schiff, James Speyer, and Cornelius Vanderbilt. The founders viewed its creation as a response to the financial panic of 1893–94 and the resulting increase in unemployment and the deterioration in the social conditions of the working class. The Society's declared purpose was to be scrupulously honest and forthright in providing customers with small collateralized low-cost loans. The founders, led by James Speyer, raised the capital for the Society by selling certificates paying up to a 6 percent annual dividend rate. The PLS commenced operation in 1894. It initially made loans at 1 percent interest per month for a 1-year period. If the collateral was not redeemed within the year, or the loan was not renewed by payment of the interest and a fraction of the principal, the collateral was sold in a public auction. The Society attempted to return any surplus to the customer.[10]

Collectively, the philanthropic pawnshops and some limited-dividend consumer finance companies were known as remedial loan societies. Under the sponsorship of the Russell Sage Foundation, the remedial loan societies started a national organization around 1910 and held occasional meetings into the 1920s. In 1932, there were 27 remedial loan societies operating in the United States; of these, only the Provident Loan Society survives. The Collateral Loan Company of Boston ceased operations sometime in the 1940s; the philanthropic First State Pawner's Society in Chicago became a regular commercial pawnshop in 1952; and the San Francisco Provident and Remedial Loan Association, founded in 1912 and patterned after the Provident Loan Society in New York City, also converted to a commercial pawnshop.

The Provident Loan Society probably survived when the others did not because it was the largest and best capitalized of the remedial loan societies, enabling it to weather years with operating losses. It also undoubtedly gained from the dense population of New York City, assuring a demand for its services even when

---

[10]By 1897 the paid-up capital of the PLS was $200,000; its average loan size was $20.80. Patterson reported that this average was at least three times that of private pawnshops, and attributed it to the fact that PLS did not lend on bulky goods, such as clothes, furniture, or tools. In addition, Patterson thought that its banklike premises and reputable image attracted better-off customers.

pawnbroking began to decline in the 1930s. It was able to offer loans at interest rates much lower than those charged by commercial pawnshops because its shareholders agreed to receive a below-market rate of return on their investment. In fact, after 1944, the PLS bought out its investors and has operated as a self-sustaining nonprofit organization ever since. The Society's costs were also lower because, as a nonprofit organization, it was tax-exempt. The PLS further reduced its costs by refusing to accept collateral with high storage costs. Throughout its history, the PLS accepted almost exclusively jewelry and other small valuable objects as collateral.

In a booklet celebrating its fiftieth anniversary, it reported that:

> Nearly one-half the borrowers are women. Jews predominate among borrowers, perhaps because they have learned, from century old experiences and environment on the Continent, to look upon the pledge loan as one of the most readily accessible sources of credit. . . . No less than 75 percent of all loans numerically, and about 95 percent measured by dollar amounts, are made on pledges of diamonds or other precious stones; the balance on a great miscellany of articles, including watches, silverware, items made of precious metals, cameras, optical goods, musical instruments, etc. [Provident Loan Society 1944, p. 27]

The PLS generally limited the number of very small loans. Given its relatively low interest rates, the transaction costs of handling small loans were higher than what the Society charged for the service and it lost money on these loans. However, because of its philanthropic orientation, the PLS always made some small loans, hoping to cover the losses on such loans through earnings on the larger loans.

The PLS continues to operate to this day. In 1991 the PLS made loans of from $25 up to $25,000 from its six locations in New York City. The loans were for a term of one year and carried an annual interest rate of 26 percent, compared to the 36 percent charged by commercial pawnbrokers in New York City. (The Society raised the annual interest rate on its loans from 23 percent in June of 1990 to eliminate an operating deficit.)

The Society made 56,428 loans in 1991, including new and renewed loans for $15,213,129, implying an average loan size of

$270. (Nationally, commercial pawnbrokers had an average loan size of about $60.) In 1991, about 16 percent of the Society's loans were for $50 or less, 47 percent for $125 or less, and 4 percent for over $1,000. About 9 percent of the collateral pledged at the PLS in 1990–1991 was forfeited (PLS 1991 *Annual Report*).

Although the commercial pawnbrokers of New York City generally resent the competition presented by the Provident Loan Society, several have survived many years providing loans at interest rates higher than that of the PLS. This is probably due to a number of factors. First, the Society operates quietly, and many potential customers are probably unaware of its presence and lower interest rates.

> In its dealings with the public, no suggestion is made of the Society's philanthropic origin and purpose, lest the implication drive from its doors those needy but self-respecting persons it most desires to help. . . . The Society has always refrained from advertising its services to the point of urging people to borrow. [Provident Loan Society *1944 Annual Report*, p. 29]

In addition, the Society is quite conservative in its valuation of customers' collateral. This apparently leads many customers to commercial pawnbrokers who will make larger loans.[11] One prominent retired New York City commercial pawnbroker wrote in his memoirs:

> Some of our stiffest competition was furnished for years by the Provident Loan Society, a nonprofit organization whose interest rates are lower than pawnbrokers'. But hockers could usually get larger loans on their possessions from our pawnshop. Whenever we were able to offer more money for collateral than a customer could get at the Provident, he seemed unbothered by the higher rate he had to pay for the use of money. [Simpson et al. 1954, p. 129]

---

[11]In discussing the *mont-de-piété* of Europe, Levine (1911, p. 29) explained that "In Europe, many municipal pawnshops are notoriously conservative with their loan to collateral ratios. . . . This has two effects. It creates a market for private brokers. It creates a secondary market for pawn tickets."

Both of these effects are apparent in New York City where commercial brokers compete with the Provident Loan Society, and several businesses offer to purchase PLS pawn tickets from customers, enabling the businesses to repay the customer's loan and claim ownership of the collateral.

THE DECLINE OF PAWNBROKING: 1930–1970

Pawnbroking entered into a period of decline beginning in the 1930s and lasting into the 1970s. The Depression had severe effects: those customers who had used pawnshops to finance discretionary spending greatly reduced their borrowing as they lost jobs or became more pessimistic about future economic prospects. Pawnshop sales declined in the downturn and the value of collateral plummeted, leading to losses on inventories. Moreover, pawnshops had to lend far less on the same collateral as compared to a few years earlier, which reduced their interest income.

Many of these factors are reflected in Figure 2.1, which shows trends from 1920 to 1940 for the amount of pawnshop credit outstanding, the number of loans outstanding, and the average loan size from the Provident Loan Society. Although the number of loans increased with the onset of the Depression, the value of the loans declined due to the fall in the average loan size. The Provident Loan Society, which was extremely well capitalized, survived the decline in earnings, but many small private pawnshops did not. Rolf Nugent (1939, pp. 380–382), in a study for the Russell Sage Foundation, estimated that aggregate pawnshop lending declined by 34 percent between 1930 and 1934.

Pawnbroking rebounded somewhat with the economic recovery, but it was constrained during World War II by government policies aimed at restricting consumer spending. After the war, pawnbroking entered into a gradual decline that persisted for about 25 years. Data on pawnbroking over this period are especially limited. Only two states, Indiana and Oregon, collected any detailed data on pawnshop operations prior to the 1980s. As shown in Figure 2.2, the number of pawnshop loans per capita in Indiana and Oregon declined markedly from 1945 to the early 1970s. Veteran pawnbrokers in other states have told me that they believe the business also declined in their communities during this period. In Hill's brief 1968 survey of pawnbroking, he reached a similar conclusion: "Pawnbroking declined rapidly after 1945; several cities lost one-third of their pawnshops within ten years" (p. 490).

The causes for the postwar decline in pawnbroking are varied. Beginning in the 1920s and 30s, middle-class and lower-middle-

Figure 2.1 / Provident Loan Society Activity: 1920–1940
(Nominal Value Index, 1920 = 100)

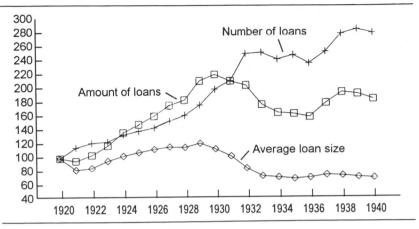

SOURCE: Provident Loan Society (1944).

class customers increasingly had access to other forms of credit. It was predicted that the rise of consumer finance companies, credit unions, and other financial institutions would hurt the pawnbroking industry:

> Competition from other lenders, such as chattel mortgage companies, salary loan concerns, industrial banks and credit

Figure 2.2 / Indiana and Oregon Pawnshop Loans per Capita: 1937–1989 (loans per 1,000 residents)

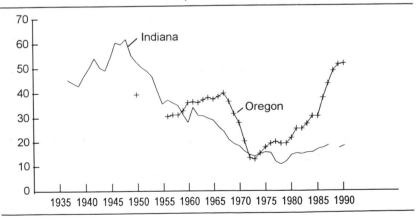

SOURCE: State regulatory agencies.

unions, has, however, become increasingly severe. . . . Where borrowing is repeated from week to week, a somewhat larger loan secured by a wage assignment and repayable in small weekly installments might be preferable. . . . [I]t is likely that pawnbroking may be entering upon a relative decline. [Kuznets 1933, p. 39]

Eight years later, Foulke concluded that after the second decade of the twentieth century, the number of pawnshops

. . . decreased very materially, probably the result of increased competition from remedial loan societies, personal loan companies, credit unions, and more recently, from the consumer loan operations of commercial banking institutions. [Foulke 1941, p. 162]

The Provident Loan Society had similar experiences. In 1944, it reported that

. . . fundamental and persistent forces have been at work restricting the Society's field of operations since the mid 30s. Throughout the growing years there was little or no competition from other types of lenders, but the last ten years have brought about a tremendous expansion in personal lending facilities. The field once served almost exclusively by the Society and commercial pawnbrokers, is now shared with licensed lenders, industrial banks, credit unions, and personal loan departments of commercial banks. [PLS 1944, p. 16]

The increasingly common mass production of consumer goods and the shift of consumer expenditures toward automobiles and bulky electronic items also contributed to the decline of pawnbroking. Mass-produced consumer items marketed through discount stores were generally too inexpensive to serve as collateral for pawnshop loans. Radios, television sets, and stereos did serve as collateral; but it was costly for the pawnshops to store them, and their value fell rapidly over time as models improved and styling changed. Kuznets, for example, claimed that "The habit of hoarding is rapidly disappearing even among the poor; the surplus above current expenditure, if not deposited with a savings institution, is more likely to be invested in a radio set, an automobile, house furniture and fixtures than in articles which might conveniently be pledged" (1933, p. 39). And 35 years later, Hill reported that "After 1945 discount houses cut into pawnbrokers' loan and sales departments, forcing lower loan valuations on pledges and lower prices in their retail trade" (1968, p. 490).

Other factors, which probably contributed to the postwar decline in pawnbroking, include rising personal incomes and the increasing generosity and scope of public-welfare programs, developments which undoubtedly reduced the need for some households to turn to pawnshops in desperation. In addition, several veteran pawnbrokers told me in interviews that increasing urban crime levels and racial tensions prompted many inner-city brokers in the 1960s to abandon pawnbroking. They also said that expanded professional opportunities and the stigma associated with pawnbroking led the sons and daughters of many brokers of the 1950s and 1960s to become professionals or enter other businesses, rather than follow their parents into pawnbroking.[12]

THE EVOLUTION OF COMMERCIAL CHECK CASHING

The core business of check-cashing outlets is to cash customers' paychecks or government benefit checks at a discount to the face value of the check. In addition, many CCOs cash personal checks. In some states, CCOs make "payday" loans, meaning that they cash a customer's personal check with the understanding that it will not be cleared through the banking system until the customer can deposit his next paycheck, perhaps a week or two hence. Such an agreement is obviously a short-term consumer loan, but some check cashers claim that it is merely a delayed check-cashing transaction and should not fall under the laws governing consumer loans.

The first commercial check-cashing outlets opened in the 1930s, but there are some earlier historical antecedents to the business.

---

[12] There was also a dramatic decline in pawnbroking in Great Britain during this period. As reported by A. L. Minkes, in 1913 there were 5,087 licensed pawnshops in Great Britain. By 1950, there were only 1,654. He concluded that: "The broad explanations of the decreased importance of [British] pawnbroking are, on the demand side, the great extension of the scope of social policy, the maintenance of continued full employment, and changes in the opportunities and attitudes of consumers, and on the supply side the declining relative attractiveness of pawnbroking as an occupation" (Minkes 1953, p. 21).

Before the Civil War, for example, banks printed their own paper currencies, called "bank notes," which were accepted as a means for payment because each bank promised to exchange on demand a note that it printed for gold or silver coins (specie). In order to initiate this exchange, however, customers would have to appear in the bank's lobby with the notes they desired to redeem. If the bank that issued the currency was not conveniently located, this increased the cost to a customer of redeeming the notes. Moreover, there was always some risk that the issuing bank would fail and would be unable to redeem its currency. In this environment, businesses arose that would convert consumers' bank notes into specie for a fee. The operators of these businesses were called "note brokers," and they would buy customers' bank notes at a discount to the face value of the note (Hammond 1957). The discount covered the broker's cost of redeeming the notes and the risk that some notes would be unredeemable. Bank notes issued by more distant or less well capitalized banks were subject to higher discounts.

Early check-clearing procedures of banks are another historical antecedent to the activities of check-cashing outlets. Prior to the creation of the Federal Reserve System in 1913, many banks did not clear at par checks written by their depositors. Under this system, for example, a bank's depositor might write a check to a person living in another city. The recipient of the check would present the check to her bank to have payment credited to her account. The bank on which the check was drawn would then forward to the recipient's bank an amount less than the full face value of the check. The discount was to cover the bank's cost of transmitting the money to the recipient's bank. Financial historians report, however, that the charge ". . . in many instances was excessive and bore no relation to any cost in connection with having funds at the desired point" (Catanach 1939, p. 25). In 1916 the Federal Reserve outlawed non-par remittance by its member banks and the practice died out.

There are also historical precedents to "payday" loans. At the turn of the century, many states had highly restrictive usury laws that prevented legitimate small-loan companies from operating. To evade these laws, some unlicensed lenders began to structure their consumer loans as "salary-purchase" agreements (Neifeld

1939, pp. 37–39). In such an agreement, the lender "buys" the borrower's wages at a discount in advance of the borrower's payday. Lenders argued that these transactions were property purchases and did not fall under the usury laws. The Uniform Small Loan Laws, which many states adopted between 1916 and 1935 at the urging of the Russell Sage Foundation, defined salary buying as cash lending, thereby subjecting it to small loan regulations. These same laws also raised the usury ceilings for small consumer loans, permitting the development of a licensed consumer finance industry.

The origin of commercial check-cashing outlets was linked to the rising use of checks for paying salaries. Although checks have been used in the United States since the early nineteenth century, they did not become common until after the Civil War, and even then, they were almost exclusively used for payments between businesses. It is unclear when checks became a common means of paying workers. However, some evidence and informal interviews with retired workers suggest that many firms began to pay middle-income workers by check in the 1910s and 20s, possibly prompted by increasingly stringent tax and bookkeeping requirements.[13] By the 1950s, the payment of wages by check was common, even for lower-income workers. This payment practice continued through the 1980s. The Federal Reserve Board's Survey of Currency and Transaction Account Usage (Avery et al. 1986, pp. 102–103) showed that in 1984 about 5 percent of employees were paid in cash, 14 percent were paid by an automatic transfer to their bank accounts, and 71 percent were paid by check. As the percentage of workers paid by check increased between the 1920s and the 1980s, the demand for a convenient means to cash those checks grew, especially by those without bank accounts. In addition, increasingly comprehensive social security and welfare systems led to large increases in the decade following World War II in the number of people receiving government support checks.

---

[13]Lizabeth Cohen. *Making A New Deal* 1990, p. 79. I am grateful to Viviana Zelizer for the Cohen reference. I spoke with several people in their eighties and nineties who remembered receiving salaries in cash tucked into pay envelopes. In fact, Sacco and Vanzetti were convicted of robbing and killing the paymaster of the Slater and Morrill Shoe Factory for $15,776 in cash in 1920. These cash holdings were to be used by the firm to pay its workers.

Prior to the development of CCOs, workers could cash their paychecks at their own banks if they had sufficient funds in their accounts to cover the checks, or they could deposit the checks and wait for them to clear. Workers without bank accounts, or those with accounts who did not choose to cash the checks at their own banks, might cash them at the banks on which they were drawn or might ask a retail store to cash their checks. Among the retail businesses willing to cash third-party checks were groceries, department stores, drugstores, and bars, which rarely levied fees for the service because they expected the cost of the service to be covered by the additional sales it might generate. Some stores limited their check-cashing service to regular customers or to customers who made minimum required purchases.

These arrangements served most workers reasonably well and continue to do so. However, many groceries or department stores in large cities were reluctant to cash paychecks for fear of fraud, for fear that the check would not clear, or because they did not have sufficient cash on hand.

Consequently, there was a market for fee-based check cashing. Although there appear to be no historical records on the origin of commercial check-cashing outlets, veteran check cashers cite a variety of causes for the rise of the business. Their most convincing explanation is that CCOs first appeared in Chicago and New York City in the 1930s—in Chicago, apparently because many neighborhoods were without bank services due to Illinois' unit banking laws and the failure of numerous banks in the Depression. This rationale agrees with that offered by the Illinois Department of Financial Institutions, which states in its *Annual Report* (1980, p. 60) that check-cashing firms, ". . . came into being during the 'Great Depression' of the 1930s. [They] became necessary when a great number of banks failed in the local community and the public still needed to be provided with banking type services."

In a study of the check-cashing business in New York City, Irving Wolf traces the origin of CCOs to changes in payment practices in the garment industry. In the early twentieth century, garment manufacturers provided a design and basic materials to small-scale contractors, who hired low-wage workers to cut and sew the garments. Since the contractors generally had little capital or borrowing power, the manufacturers paid the contractors in cash weekly, and they in turn paid their workers weekly. Sometime in the 1920s, some garment manufacturers began to pay contractors by check. Since the contractors felt that they had to pay their workers in cash immediately, the contractors could not deposit the checks in banks and wait for them to clear: they had to cash the checks right away. According to Wolf, this service was initially provided by a local saloonkeeper, who cashed the checks if the contractors would purchase a few drinks. By the 1930s, however, demand outgrew the liquid capital of the saloonkeeper. In response, entrepreneurs with sufficient capital offered to cash checks, but charged an explicit fee for the service. In the 1940s and 1950s, as more and more businesses began to pay their workers with checks, check-cashing outlets opened throughout New York City.

Commercial check cashing grew strongly in Chicago and New York City and was well entrenched in these cities by the early 1970s. Elsewhere, however, the industry generally failed to gain more than a toehold. Established check cashers in Philadelphia told me that CCOs first opened there in the 1940s, started by entrepreneurs who had seen CCOs in Chicago. By the late 1960s, however, only a handful were operating in the city. Statements from check cashers in other cities indicate that CCOs existed only in the 5 or 6 largest urban areas until the early 1970s, when they began to appear gradually in cities throughout the country. Many were apparently started by Chicago check cashers who thought that the business should have potential in other cities. In some cases, CCOs evolved from nonfinancial retail businesses that also cashed checks.

Undoubtedly due to Chicago's influence, CCOs also spread to a few Canadian cities by the late 1970s. Otherwise, they appear to be a uniquely American phenomenon. This is probably due to several factors. First, in some other countries it is still common for moderate and low-wage workers to be paid in cash.[14] Second, in countries where a large share of the workers are unionized, unions often negotiate with employers to have paychecks cashed

---

[14]In the United Kingdom, for example, 37 percent of adult employees were paid in cash in 1984 (Kirkman 1987, p. 113).

by the employer at the work site. Third, outside of the United States, post offices commonly serve as low-cost convenient deposit institutions for moderate-income households, raising the percentage of the population who have deposit accounts. Finally, it is common in other countries for just a few large bank chains to dominate the financial system, making it easier for people to cash their paychecks at a branch of the bank on which they are drawn.

3 / Contemporary Fringe Banking

From 1930 through the mid-1970s, the pawnbroking industry contracted. Over this same period, the check-cashing industry grew, but remained largely confined to Chicago, New York City, and a small number of other urban areas. Beginning in the mid-1970s, however, these fringe banking industries grew explosively. In absolute numbers, or measured on a per capita basis, there are more pawnshops today than at any time in the history of the United States. Florida and Texas each have more than 1,000 pawnshops, which combined make more than an estimated ten million loans annually. Over the 1980s, check-cashing outlets opened in cities all across the country. In just the past 5 years, the number of CCOs throughout the country doubled, rising from about 2,000 outlets to almost 5,000.

Such rapid growth is initially puzzling, considering that fringe banking services are far more costly than the comparable services of mainstream financial institutions. In many states, for example, pawnshop interest rates are over 200 percent a year. Similarly, the cost of obtaining basic payment services through a CCO is commonly four to ten times higher than similar bank services.

The following chapters attempt to resolve this puzzle. Before doing so, however, it is important to understand how contemporary pawnshops and CCOs operate, the fees they levy for their services, and the regulations governing their behavior. This chapter addresses these topics, documents the 1980s boom in fringe banking, and discusses the rise of national fringe-banking chains.

CONTEMPORARY PAWNBROKING

As pawnbrokers have done for centuries, the contemporary pawnbroker makes fixed term loans to customers based on the value of the collateral they leave in the possession of the broker. A customer might, for example, bring in a watch with a $100 retail value and leave it as collateral for a $50 loan due to be repaid in two months. Pawnshop customers, however, have no legal obligation to repay the loans. If they do not, the pawnbroker becomes the owner of the collateral and the debt is extinguished. Alternatively, the customers can redeem the pledged collateral at any time within the term of the loan and stipulated grace period. To do so, they repay the principal and pay the interest and any other required fees on the loan. In this sense, a pawnshop loan is equivalent to an options market transaction, where the broker purchases the collateral but the customer retains the option to repurchase the item within a specified time period at an agreed-upon price. Because the majority of customers redeem their pledges, the main function of pawnshops is to provide small, secured, short-term consumer loans.

Contemporary U.S. pawnshops are regulated by state and, sometimes, by local governments. These regulations vary, but there is a general pattern: when someone pawns a good, the terms of the loan contract must be specified on a pawn ticket; the ticket states the customer's name and address, a description of the pledged good, the amount lent, the maturity date, and the amount that must be paid to redeem the good. The broker keeps a copy of the pawn ticket, the customer receives a copy, and a copy must be filed with the local police. When the customer is ready to redeem the item, he or she presents the ticket along with the amount owed, and the broker returns the collateral.

In response to the popular belief that pawnshops serve as fences for burglars, all brokers that I interviewed adamantly insisted that they do not knowingly accept stolen goods as collateral. Although one would expect even dishonest brokers to make such a claim, I found the brokers' explanation generally convincing. They argued that it is not in their interest to make loans on stolen goods because the police can seize the goods, and the broker would lose the collateral and the money loaned. Given the police report requirement, they also said that it would not be in the interest of a thief to pawn stolen goods, and many charged that stolen goods are far more commonly channelled through unregulated flea markets. Although many items, especially jewelry, do not have serial numbers and would be difficult to identify from police reports, available data support the brokers' claims. For example, Oklahoma state officials report that in 1991 the police seized less than 0.1 percent of pawned goods as being stolen property.

Most states set ceilings on the interest rate and other fees, such as those for storage or insurance, that pawnshops can charge on loans. Including these fees, ceiling rates for pawnshop loans range from 1.5 percent a month to 25 percent a month of the amount of the loan. No state allows compounding of the interest rate. Some states impose no ceilings. In several states, the ceiling rate depends on the size of the loan. In Oklahoma, for example, a pawnshop can levy a 20 percent monthly interest rate on a loan up to $150, a 15 percent monthly interest rate on that amount over $150 but less than $250, and so on.

Table 3.1 presents the legal ceilings on interest rates and other fees for pawnshop loans in a selection of states. To permit interstate comparisons, the interest rates and fees presented in the table are for a $55 loan outstanding 2 months, a typical loan for most pawnshops. In states such as Illinois, which permit a service fee and do not specify a minimum maturity period, pawnshops can increase the effective annual interest rate by making one-month loans and imposing a new service fee each time the loans are renewed.[1] Where ceilings on pawnshop rates are 20 percent

---

[1] From the customer's point of view, it makes no difference whether a pawnshop calls the fees on loans an "interest rate," a "storage cost," or something else. All that matters to the customer is the amount that must be paid for the advance of the principal. This justifies the inclusion of storage and other fees into the calculation of the effective annual interest rate in Table 3.1. This does not imply, however, that pawn-

a month, pawnshops almost universally charge the ceiling rate on loans of less than $100, which are the vast majority of their loans. In some states, where the ceiling rate is below 10 percent a month and enforcement is lax, almost all pawnshops charge more than the legal maximum. For instance, in Mississippi prior to 1993, pawnbrokers could legally charge less than $3 for a 1-month $50 loan, but brokers commonly charged at least $10 for such loans.[2] In other states, deviations from the law are more limited. For example, in 1989 I pawned a VCR for $35 at a Philadelphia pawnshop and was issued a ticket showing that in order to redeem it I would need to pay $1.50 in finance charges, the maximum legal fee for a one-month loan of this size. When I went to redeem the item, however, I was informed that I would need to pay another $1.00 for "insurance," an illegal additional charge.

Where pawnshop fees are unregulated, as in Florida, Iowa, and South Dakota, or where the legal ceiling is well above 20 percent a month, a small telephone survey that I conducted in 1989 found that most pawnshops were charging between 18 and 28 percent a month for a loan of $50. This suggests that the unregulated market rate on a typical pawnshop loan is at least a 240 percent annual percentage rate (APR).

Most states regulate the maturity of pawnshop loans, typically requiring pawnbrokers to make loans with 1- to 3-month maturities. There is also a legally required grace period, commonly from 1–3 months, during which time the broker must hold the collateral after the term of the loan expires. During the grace period, the customer maintains the right to redeem the collateral, although the interest owed on the loan continues to accumulate. Customers can generally renew loans indefinitely by paying the interest and other fees due on the loan at maturity. Brokers report that many pledges are redeemed within a week or two. In such cases, how-

---

shop fees and interest rates simply represent the time value of money to the broker. Rather, they mainly cover the broker's fixed costs of running the shop and the transaction cost of making a loan.

[2] To veil the legal violation, many brokers in Mississippi structured their loans as purchases, with the seller retaining the right to repurchase the item anytime up to a specified date at a stated price. In the slang of pawnbrokers, this is known as a "buy-sell" agreement and is identical to a pawnshop loan in all aspects except the terminology. In 1993, Mississippi revised its laws to permit brokers to charge a monthly interest rate of up to 25 percent of the amount lent, removing the incentive for pawnbrokers to attempt to evade the law through buy-sell agreements.

Table 3.1 / State Pawnshop Regulations: As of End 1991

State	Maximum Interest Rate Charge on $55 Loan Outstanding 2 Months	Maximum Other Fees on $55 Loan Outstanding 2 Months	Effective Maximum Annual Interest Rate
Alabama[a]	NL	NL	NL
California	$7.50	$0.00	82%
Florida[b]	NL	NL	NL
Georgia[c]	$5.00	$27.50	355%
Illinois[d]	$3.30	$12.00	167%
Indiana[e]	$3.30	$3.00	69%
New York	$3.30	$0.00	36%
North Carolina[f]	$2.20	$22.00	264%
Oklahoma	$22.00	$0.00	240%
Oregon	$3.30	$5.00	91%
Pennsylvania	$0.55	$2.75	36%
Texas	$22.00	$0.00	240%
Wyoming	$22.00	$0.00	240%

SOURCES: State regulatory agencies, American Business Information Inc., and Statistical Abstract of the U.S.

NOTE: NL: no statutory limit.

[a]In December 1992, Alabama set a maximum charge of 25 percent of principal per month on the combined total of pawnshop interest rates and other fees.
[b]Florida laws are for "buy-sell" transactions, which is the way most pawn loans are structured.
[c]Prior to 1989, pawnshops in Georgia could not levy "other" fees on loans. A small telephone survey indicated that the "effective" annual interest rate ceiling in Georgia is not binding.
[d]Prior to 1991, pawnshops in Illinois could not levy "other" fees on loans. The grace period in Illinois can be shortened with the permission of the customer. Shortening the grace period raises the effective interest rate on longer-term loans, since the shops levy a fee on loan initiations and renewals.
[e]The maximum monthly charge for storage fees on a $55 loan in Indiana was raised from $1.50 to 20 percent of the principal on 7/1/92.
[f]Prior to 1990, pawnshops in North Carolina could not levy "other" fees on loans.

ever, the customer must pay a full month's interest. A typical pledge, according to brokers, is redeemed within 2–3 months.

In the case of nonredemption, after the grace period has expired, the collateral becomes the property of the pawnshop. The broker can then sell it on a retail basis from the shop or sell it wholesale to a used goods dealer. Some states require that the

Minimum Maturity Period (in months)	Minimum Grace Period (in months)	Surplus Must Be Returned to Customer?	Number of Residents per Pawnshop Outlet	Approximate Number Pawnshop Outlets
2	0	no	13,035	310
4	0.3	no	58,353	510
2	0	no	10,187	1270
1	0.3	no	8,935	725
NL	12	no	114,310	100
NL	3	yes	158,400	35
6	0	yes	359,800	50
1	2	no	18,940	350
1	1	no	8,503	370
3	1	no	203,000	14
NL	3	yes	198,033	60
1	2	no	15,235	1115
1	0	no	9,080	50

collateral be sold at public auction. Thirteen states and the District of Columbia require that any surplus from the sale of the collateral, over the amount owed the pawnbroker including accumulated interest and any costs related to the sale, revert to the customer. But most brokers admit that it is a rare customer who ever sees any surplus returned. In some cases this is because the broker underreports the sale price of the collateral or makes no effort to notify the customer of the surplus.[3] When brokers do try to return the surplus, they say that they often cannot locate their customers, many of whom may have pawned the item several months or a year ago and moved since or may have given a false address when pawning it. Nonredemption rates of 10–30 percent are typical in the states for which there are data.[4]

---

[3]For example, William Simpson, a prominent retired pawnbroker from New York City, recalled in his memoirs, "Concerning the equity that should go to the original hocker after the auction sales, I am not going to pretend that Simpson's or any other pawnbroker ever blew bugles and threw out dragnets to find the hockers" (Simpson et al. 1954, p. 140).

[4]Pawn tickets are legally transferable in most states, so it is hard to know the true nonredemption rate. In New York City, for example, pawnshops report average forfeit

A broker lends a customer a percentage of the value the broker believes the collateral would bring in a sale. The loan to collateral ratio varies over time and across pawnshops, but a loan of about 50 percent of the resale value of the collateral is common. For example, the VCR that I pawned in 1989 had been purchased new for $220 about 6 months earlier. After some haggling, the broker was willing to lend me $35 on the VCR. Given that a used VCR in good condition would have probably sold quickly for around $70, the $35 loan fits these rough guidelines.

With about a 50 percent loan to collateral ratio, the broker almost always makes a one-time gain if the customer fails to redeem the collateral. Brokers say, however, that they prefer customers to redeem their collateral. A customer who loses his or her collateral may feel bitter towards the shop and patronize another, and brokers claim they would prefer to lend repeatedly to a customer rather than profit once from the forfeit. Pawnbrokers report that about 70 to 80 percent of their customers are repeat customers.

To provide some idea of the quantitative aspects of pawnshop operations, Table 3.2 presents 1990 data from three state regulatory agencies and from a recent annual report of Cash America International, Inc., a company with a chain of pawnshops whose stock is traded on the New York Stock Exchange. These three states, especially Indiana and Oregon, provide more detail than any others on pawnshop operations. In examining the data, one should keep in mind that many pawnbrokers may underreport their activity to tax authorities and state regulators since it is a cash-based business. The data for Cash America are probably more reliable because it is an audited, publicly traded firm. However, Cash America's pawnshops may not be representative of pawnshops nationally because they are probably better capitalized than most, allowing them to make more loans. On the other hand, Cash America's shops are concentrated in states with liberal usury ceilings, where pawnshops are numerous and operate on a smaller scale than average.

---

rates below 10 percent. However, there are also yellow-page listings in New York by businesses willing to buy a customer's pledge ticket. The ticket has value if the pledged item is worth more than the principal and interest needed to redeem it. In no other city have I seen similar public offers to buy pawn tickets, and reported forfeit rates for most states probably only slightly underrepresent actual default rates.

Table 3.2 / Selected Pawnshop Financial Data: 1990

	Indiana	Oklahoma	Oregon	Cash America
Beginning of Year				
Number licensed pawnshops	32	377	13	123
Number loans outstanding	43,050	NA	35,087	308,354
Amount loans outstanding	$2,271,194	NA	$2,377,460	$20,043,000
Year End				
Number licensed pawnshops	32	388	14	151
Number loans outstanding	47,578	NA	36,243	332,929
Amount loans outstanding	$2,631,723	NA	$2,673,753	$23,305,000
Per shop number loans outstanding	1,487	NA	2,589	2,205
Per shop amount loans outstanding	$82,241	NA	$190,982	$154,338
Over the Year				
Number loans made and renewed	100,339	1,165,008	146,880	1,751,689
Amount loans made and renewed	$5,337,503	$62,891,202	$10,149,716	$118,239,000
Number loans forfeited	17,132	356,270	18,825	NA
Amount loans forfeited	$736,637	$13,064,018	$840,370	$38,751,000
Total pawn fees collected	$1,071,038	$14,715,979	$1,017,789	$44,486,000
Avg. size loan made and renewed	$53.19	$53.98	$69.10	$70.00
Number forfeited as percentage of number of loans made and renewed	17.1%	30.6%	12.8%	NA
Amount forfeited as percentage of amount of loans made and renewed	13.8%	20.8%	8.3%	32.8%
Implied average annual interest rate on loans outstanding	43.7%	NA	40.3%	205.3%
Per shop number loans made and renewed	3,136	3,046	10,880	12,786
Per shop amount loans made and renewed	$166,797	$164,421	$751,831	$863,058

SOURCES: State regulatory agencies, Cash America International, Inc., and author's estimates.

NOTE: Data on number of Cash America loans are author's estimates based on company's reported average loan size.

Keeping these qualifications in mind, one notes in the table that these pawnshops each had about 1,500–2,500 loans outstanding at the time they filed their reports. Over the year, however, they made or renewed about two to six times this number of loans. This turnover rate will vary across states based on the minimum legal loan term, grace period, and other factors. The nonredemption rate, measured by the value of loans made, varied between 8 and 33 percent. The nonredemption rate, measured by the number of loans made, was somewhat higher, indicating that a larger percentage of small pledges are forfeited than are large ones. One might expect the nonredemption rate to be higher in states with relatively high interest rates, and this pattern holds in the table.

The average loan size in 1990 for the pawnshops in Table 3.2 was between $50 and $70. The average is probably higher in states that require pawnshops to charge less than 5 percent a month in interest and fees, for pawnshops in these states often refuse to make loans for less than $25 because the transaction costs exceed the permitted fees. However, at most pawnshops, the vast majority of loans in 1990 were certainly for less than $100. In Indiana, for example, out of the 100,339 loans made by 32 pawnshops in 1990, 93 percent were for less than $100 and 76 percent were for less than $50 (Figure 3.1). As this indicates, the median pawnshop loan is significantly smaller than the mean.

Throughout the country, commonly pawned items include jewelry, electronic and photographic equipment, musical instruments, and firearms. These items maintain their value over a reasonable period of time and are easy to store, especially jewelry. Examination of police records in Wilmington, Delaware, for example, showed that over an 8-day period in 1989 one pawnshop made 221 loans for a total amount of $10,790. The average loan size was $46, and the range of loans fell between $5 and $500. Of the items pledged, 68 percent consisted of watches and jewelry; 21 percent television, stereo, or video equipment; 4 percent musical instruments; 2.7 percent camera equipment; and 2.7 percent firearms. A few states regulate the type of items that can be pawned. An interesting example is Delaware, where it is illegal for a pawnbroker to accept a customer's artificial limb as collateral.

At the turn of the century, many pawnshops took winter coats as collateral for loans. Customers would pawn the coats in the

Figure 3.1 / Distribution of Indiana Pawnshop Loans, by Size: 1990

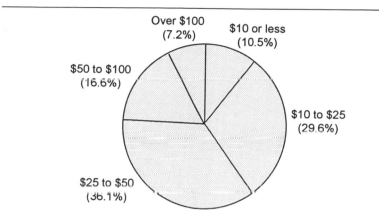

SOURCE: Indiana Department of Financial Institutions.

spring and redeem them in the fall. Although pawnshops no longer accept clothing as collateral, there are modern equivalents of such seasonal practices. Some pawnshops in Philadelphia, for example, take window air conditioning units in pawn in the fall. Customers redeem the units in the early summer.

The Growth and Size of the Pawnbroking Industry

Following the decline in pawnbroking that began in the 1930s, the industry staged a remarkable turnaround starting around the mid-1970s and centered in Southern and Central Mountain states. Unfortunately, there are no data on pawnbroking in most states prior to the 1970s. However, veteran pawnbrokers in the South have told me that the industry in their states grew sluggishly in the 1950s and 60s and then boomed from the late 1970s through the 80s. This is consistent with what little official data are available. For example, state regulators in Texas report that there were 375 licensed pawnshops in the state in 1968. By 1975 there were 529, and by 1990 there were 1,329. In Oklahoma there were 212 licensed pawnshops in 1978. By 1991 there were 397, making 1.3 million loans a year or about 4 loans for every 10 residents.

In states outside of the South and Central Mountain region,

there are far fewer pawnshops, and the growth in pawnbroking appears to have been much more moderate. In Pennsylvania, for example, state regulators report that there were 29 licensed pawnshops in 1978. This number stayed fairly constant until 1985 when new shops began to open. By 1991 there were 57 licensed pawnshops. Official data from Oregon and Indiana show that pawnshop lending declined from the 1940s and 1950s through the mid-1970s (see Figure 2.2). It subsequently recovered modestly in Indiana and rapidly in Oregon. In contrast to these states, the data from New Jersey show no sign of a recovery in pawnbroking. In 1950, there were 33 licensed pawnshops in the state. By 1985 there were 15, and the number was unchanged in 1991.

The rapid growth shown in Texas and Oklahoma was apparently characteristic of the growth in most Southern states as well as in a few states outside of the region. In fact, national trends in the 1980s were dominated by the trends in the states with large and rapidly growing numbers of pawnshops. Although there are no official national data, American Business Information, a firm that compiles lists of businesses in the classified pages of telephone books, indicated that in late 1985, the earliest period for which it provided data, there were 4,849 pawnshops listed nationwide.[5] By early 1992, there were 8,787.[6] The 1985–92 trend in yellow-page listings across the nation is illustrated in Figure 3.2.

---

[5] I am grateful to Kristin Lewis of American Business Information for providing these data.

[6] A comparison of the number of pawnshop outlets listed in the classified pages of telephone books with the number reported by state regulators shows a generally close correspondence. Only a few state regulators report pawnshop data, and these are indicated below:

	End-1990 Official Count	End-1990 Yellow-Page Count
Indiana	32	34
New Jersey	15	24
Oklahoma	388	328
Oregon	14	17
Pennsylvania	63	45
Texas	1,329	991

Discrepancies may be explained by differences in timing of the counts, differences between the number of licenses outstanding and actual operating shops, mistakes by state regulators or the assemblers of the yellow-page count, and the choice of some pawnbrokers not to list their businesses in the classified pages.

Figure 3.2 / Yellow-Page Listings of Pawnshops: 1986–1992

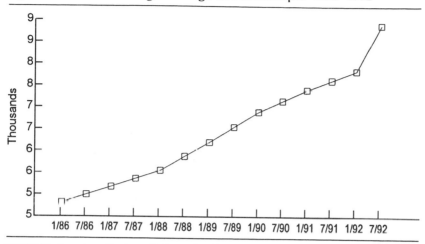

SOURCE: American Business Information Inc.

Because of the skewed growth pattern, pawnbroking today is centered in the South (Figure 3.3). The classified pages of telephone books in early 1992 list, for example, 1,274 pawnshops in Florida, 1,115 in Texas, 744 in Georgia, 512 in California, 364 in Oklahoma, 356 in North Carolina, 341 in Mississippi, and 317 in Alabama. These numbers stand in striking contrast to the 45 listed in New York, 42 in Connecticut, 27 in Massachusetts, and 25 in Wisconsin.

Thus, contrary to many people's beliefs, pawnbroking has not died out. Rather, it has expanded and relocated from the older major urban areas, primarily in the Northeast, to the South and Central Mountain region. As noted in the previous chapter, Samuel Levine estimated that in 1911 there were 1,976 licensed pawnbrokers in the country, or about one for every 47,500 inhabitants, and he noted that they were concentrated in the major urban areas of the Northeast. Today, there are almost 9,000 pawnshops, or about one for every 28,360 U.S. residents, and they are regularly found in cities with as few as 10,000 inhabitants as well as in major urban areas throughout the country.

There are no official estimates of the aggregate amount of credit provided by pawnshops in the United States. The Federal Reserve System does not collect data on pawnbroking and does not in-

Figure 3.3 / Pawnshops per Million Inhabitants, by State: As of End 1989

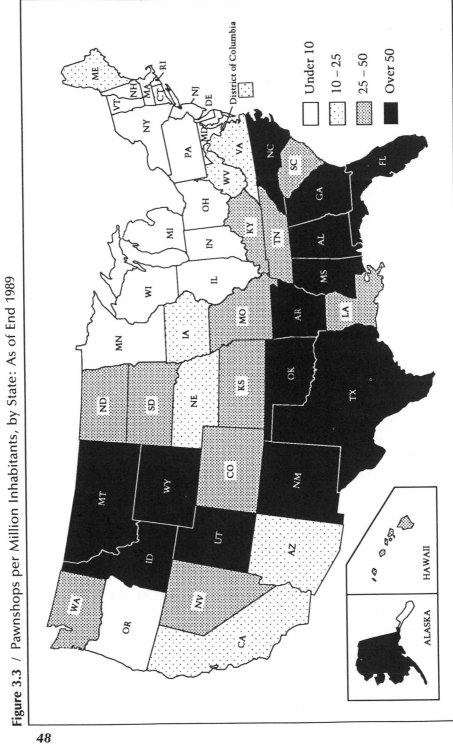

SOURCE: Caskey and Zikmund (1990).

clude an estimate of pawnshop credit in its statistics on total do-
mestic credit. However, extrapolating from the data provided by
a few state regulatory agencies and Cash America Investments, I
estimate that total pawnshop credit outstanding at the end of
1991 was around $660 million, with pawnshops making about $3.3
billion of loans over the year.[7]

These estimates suggest that pawnshops provide significantly
less than one percent of consumer credit in the United States. By
other measures, however, pawnbroking plays an important role
in U.S. credit markets. The data suggest, for example, that pawnshops made about 42 million loans in 1991. Even allowing for
multiple loans to a core group of customers, pawnshops clearly
serve several million Americans each year, perhaps as much as
10 percent of the adult population and well over 10 percent in
several states. However, since the median loan is only about
$60, pawnshop lending as a percentage of total consumer credit
is much less significant than as a percentage of the population
served.

Explaining the Concentration of Pawnshops in the South and Central Mountain Region

The most important reason for the concentration of pawnshops
in the Southern and Central Mountain states is the more liberal
usury laws in these states. To understand why high interest rate
ceilings increase the number of pawnshops, consider two key fea-
tures of the industry. First, pawnbroking is characterized by high
customer transportation costs relative to the size of the transaction. To obtain a loan or redeem collateral, a customer must physi-

[7]Because data are scarce and pawnshop operations vary widely across states, it is
impossible to obtain a precise estimate of the magnitude of pawnshop operations
nationally. As a general rule, pawnshops in states with lower legal interest rate ceilings
or longer minimum loan periods must maintain a larger number of loans outstanding
than pawnshops in other states if they are to survive. However, over two-thirds of all
pawnshops nationally are located in states where they levy fees of 15 percent a month
or more and make 1- or 2-month loans. Therefore, my estimate of the size of the
industry assumes a fairly small, average scale operation. For the estimates reported in
the text, I assumed that there were 8,780 pawnshops operating in the U.S. in 1991
and that the average pawnshop had 1,200 pledge loans outstanding at the end of 1991
with an average loan size of $62. I also assumed that the typical pawnshop made
about 4,800 new loans over the year.

cally transport the collateral to or from the pawnshop. With an average loan of around $60, transportation costs per dollar of credit are significant, and customers generally patronize the closest shop. Second, barriers to entry into pawnbroking are generally small. Almost all states require brokers to pay a small annual license fee. Some states will not issue licenses to applicants with felony criminal records; otherwise a license is generally available to anyone able to pay the fee. In most locations, a pawnshop outlet can be started with an investment of between $50,000 and $150,000, placing start-up costs within reach of many entrepreneurs (Fletcher 1992 and Gregory and Norton 1985).[8]

These characteristics explain why differences in usury laws are the main factor behind the skewed distribution of pawnshops across the states. Generous usury laws permit small-scale pawnshops to operate profitably, and high customer transportation costs mean that they will be patronized. Because of the low barriers to entry, entrepreneurs who recognize a demand for pawnshop services can open new shops to meet that demand.

In addition to usury laws, the number of pawnshops per capita is affected by regulations governing loan maturities and the allocation of any surplus from the sale of forfeited collateral. The shorter the loan maturity and the grace period, the better for pawnbrokers. Where state laws allow brokers to charge one-time transaction fees on loans, longer maturity periods effectively lower the rate pawnshops can charge. Moreover, some items in storage depreciate over time, decreasing pawnshop gains in case of non-redemption or decreasing the amount brokers can lend on collateral. State regulations that require pawnbrokers to return any surplus from the sale of a forfeited pledge to the customer are disadvantageous to the brokers. Were states with such laws to enforce them rigorously, it would undoubtedly limit the size of the industry in these states.

Finally, the number of pawnshops in a state is likely to be related to the percentage of families with low incomes and below-average education levels. The higher the percentage of house-

---

[8]Entry costs vary by state. The amount of capital required to start a pawnshop depends on the length of time for which loans are made and the class of collateral in which the shop deals. The longer the loan period or the higher the average loan balance, the more capital is required.

holds with these characteristics, the greater the demand for pawn-shop services and the more pawnshops per capita.

Reduced form regression analysis supports these conclusions. In two recent articles (Caskey and Zikmund 1990 and Caskey 1991), I examined the empirical links between the number of pawnshops per capita in 28 states and key pawnshop regulations. The regression results from the more recent article are shown in Table 3.3. In the regression, the dependent variable is the number

Table 3.3 / Regression Study of Pawnshops per Million State Residents

	Estimated Coefficient	Mean Value
Dependent Variable: PPM		29.2
Explanatory Variables		
INT	420 (6.6)	9.0
SUR	9.6 (1.2)	0.39
POV	253 (2.0)	13.4
ED	177 (3.1)	30.9
POP	−0.002 (1.0)	527.6
Constant	9.2	
Number Observations: 28		R^2. 0.80

SOURCE: Caskey (1991).

NOTES: Variable Definitions
  PPM: Number of pawnshops per million state residents in the 28 states with binding interest rate ceilings.
  INT: The state's monthly interest rate cciling on a $51 loan outstanding for three months, where the interest rate includes all fees on the loan, whether labeled "interest" or "storage fee" or something else.
  SUR: A dummy variable for states with rules requiring that any surplus from the sale of the collateral be returned to the pledger.
  POV: The percentage of persons in the state below the officially defined poverty level.
  ED: The percentage of people 25 years and older in the state attaining at least 4 years of high school education.
  POP: The state's average population per square mile.

of pawnshops per million state residents in the 28 states with binding interest rate ceilings.[9] The explanatory variables include (1) the state's monthly effective interest rate ceiling on a $51 loan outstanding for 3 months, where the "effective" interest rate includes all fees on the loan, whether labeled "interest," "storage fee," or something else; (2) a dummy variable for states with rules requiring that any surplus from the sale of the collateral be returned to the pledger; (3) the percentage of people in the state below the officially defined poverty level; (4) the percentage of people 25 years and older in the state achieving at least 4 years of high school education; and (5) the state's average population per square mile. My hypothesis was that the coefficient on the interest rate variable would be positive, the coefficient on the surplus dummy would be negative, the coefficient on the poverty variable would be positive, and the coefficient on the education variable would be negative. Theoretical considerations could justify either a negative or positive coefficient on the population density variable.

As shown in Table 3.3, the estimated coefficients on the interest rate, poverty, and education variables agreed with my expectations and are statistically significant at high levels of confidence. The sign on the surplus dummy variables is not consistent with my hypothesis, but the estimated coefficient is not statistically significant. Moreover, as discussed earlier, regulations requiring a return of surplus are rarely binding. Together the explanatory variables explain about 80 percent of the variation in pawnshops per capita across the states.

The Changing Appearance and Structure of the Industry

In addition to the rapid growth in pawnbroking over the 1980s, the decade initiated a change in the physical appearance, urban location, and structure of much of the industry. The traditional pawnshop, immortalized in such films as *The Pawnbroker*, was a small store located in an urban center, cluttered with a huge vari-

---

[9]In states without binding usury ceilings, the number of pawnshops per capita might affect the prevailing interest rate as well as vice versa. Consequently, to prevent any simultaneity bias, the regression employed data only from the 28 states with binding usury ceilings.

ety of unredeemed items for sale. In the profession, such shops are known as "miscellaneous" pawnshops. These pawnshops, which comprise the vast majority in the industry, make loans on almost anything of value, and commonly make loans for as little as $10. A much smaller number of pawnshops are "upscale"— accepting only small precious items as collateral and generally making loans above $30. These pawnshops can almost always instantly be distinguished from miscellaneous pawnshops. Because they seek to serve a more affluent clientele who might be embarrassed if seen pawning a watch or jewelry, upscale pawnshops often have closed private booths in which the loan transactions take place. Moreover, they rarely publicly label themselves as pawnshops; they might call themselves jewelry stores and place a discreet sign in the window stating, "Loans." Their names also generally differ from those of miscellaneous pawnshops. While the latter tend to go by such names as Sam's Pawnshop, Lou's Loans, or The Happy Hocker, upscale pawnshops are more likely to be named Simpson and Carter or Hartley's Jewelry.

In the mid-1980s, a new style of miscellaneous pawnshop began to appear, particularly in the South and Southwest. These shops were located in lower-middle-class suburban neighborhoods, often in strip shopping centers that had fallen on hard times after the spread of enclosed shopping malls across America. The new stores tend to resemble suburban convenience stores. They are well lit and sport bright illuminated plastic signs in front. Their merchandise is organized in attractive displays, and friendly sales people are quick to greet potential customers. For security, the loan counter is almost always located in the rear of the store, as it is in the more traditional pawnshop.

Part of the impetus behind this transformation in the appearance of pawnshops undoubtedly came from the success of Cash America Investments, whose founders began to build a chain of pawnshops in Texas in 1984, emphasizing that they were bringing modern management techniques and an improved image to a business largely dominated by dingy mom-and-pop stores. Cash America's shops had big picture windows, were clean and brightly lit, and were located so as to be convenient for an automobile-traveling public. Starting with 5 pawnshops in Texas in 1984, Cash America grew to operate 178 shops in 7 states by the end of 1991. In early 1992, Cash America purchased a small British pawnshop chain, making it an international company. Cash America's initial stock offering was in January 1987 at $6.67 a share. After a 3 for 2 stock split, its shares were trading on the New York Stock Exchange at the end of 1991 for almost $20, using the ticker tape symbol PWN for "pawn." Not surprisingly, other companies are attempting to emulate Cash America's success. Although none are yet even half as big as Cash America, there are now at least 4 publicly traded pawnshop companies attempting to build regional or national chains.

In addition to the changing physical appearance of the industry, many pawnshops have begun to operate as one-stop financial centers for their customers. It is not uncommon, for example, for a pawnshop to make loans, cash checks, sell money orders, and handle customers' utility bill payments and income tax filings. If these trends continue, in a few years the typical pawnshop will be a brightly lit, clean store, displaying forfeited pledges in well-organized sales cases. It will be located along a busy road in a lower-middle-class suburban neighborhood. A brightly colored large sign in front will identify the pawnshop's affiliation with one of the major national chains. While friendly sales personnel greet people browsing through the merchandise, efficient clerks in the rear of the shop will make collateralized loans, sell money orders, cash checks, and push "instant tax refunds."

THE CONTEMPORARY CHECK-CASHING BUSINESS

Along with the boom in pawnbroking, the 1980s saw explosive growth in commercial check-cashing outlets.[10] The core business of a CCO is cashing checks for a fee, primarily customers' paychecks or government support checks. In addition, most CCOs sell money orders and make wire transfers of customers' funds. These services enable customers who do not have checking accounts to pay bills and transfer money to relatives at distant locations.

---

[10] In Indiana, Illinois, Minnesota, and Wisconsin, firms that cash customers' checks for a fee are said to be in the "currency-exchange" business. However, I prefer the more widely used term "check-cashing" business because many people assume currency exchange involves foreign currency.

A useful way to think of the check-cashing business is to view it as "unbundling" the payment and savings services offered by banks. Banks provide payment services, such as check-cashing and checkwriting privileges, to customers who maintain deposits—and almost exclusively to these customers. In this sense, banks' payment services are bundled with their savings services; the payment services cannot be purchased separately. CCOs separate these two services, offering payment services unlinked to any savings services.

Banks can cover part or all of the cost of the payment services they offer depositors by paying artificially low interest rates on customers' deposit accounts. CCOs, on the other hand, must charge an explicit fee for the payment services they provide. The fee is intended to provide the CCO owner with a profit after covering expenses, which include personnel and insurance costs as well as bank service fees and the cost of maintaining a storefront. Moreover, because the check casher advances funds on checks that must subsequently be cleared through the banking system, CCOs incur interest expenses on the funds advanced and run the risk that some cashed checks will be uncollectible because of insufficient funds or fraud.

All check-cashing outlets must work closely with at least one bank. This is because a CCO needs a bank to clear the large volume of checks the firm cashes. Moreover, most CCOs rely on bank lines of credit to meet their periodic, substantial needs for cash.

Check-cashing fees are generally stated as a percentage of the face value of the check. It is also common for check cashers to set a flat minimum fee for cashing checks with small face values. Many check cashers impose additional charges for first-time customers, justifying these additional charges as the costs of issuing identification cards or registering new customers. CCOs also levy fees for the other services they offer, such as wiring funds or providing money orders.

Because of the risk associated with advancing money on checks, many outlets cash only customers' payroll or government assistance and entitlement checks. Some CCOs also cash personal checks, although almost all charge a higher fee for this service to cover the greater risk that the check will bounce. Many CCOs that cash personal checks do so only after they have confirmed with the bank it is drawn on that there are sufficient funds in the account to cover the check.

Most CCOs derive the majority of their revenue from check-cashing fees, with modest additional earnings coming from money order sales and wire transfers.[11] However, it is also common for CCOs to offer a number of other products. In some states, for example, CCOs sell lottery tickets and public transportation passes and distribute welfare payments and food stamps. In addition, some offer income-tax preparation services, and many sell cigarettes and candy and buy and sell gold jewelry. Because check-cashing customers receive a lump sum of cash, it is natural for CCOs to carry a range of items customers might purchase on impulse.

In some states, CCOs make so-called payday loans. They do this by cashing a customer's personal check, which is sometimes postdated, and agreeing to hold it until the customer's payday. Check cashers charge much higher fees for this service and offer it only to customers with stable employment records who have maintained bank accounts in good standing for several months, for it essentially amounts to making an unsecured loan. In most states that regulate CCOs, it is illegal for check cashers to make such loans. In states that do not regulate CCOs, payday loans are often effectively illegal because the fees violate state usury laws, the CCOs fail to obtain required small-loan licenses, or the CCOs fail to comply with federal regulations covering the disclosure of interest rates.[12]

As of the beginning of 1993, 11 states regulated the activities of CCOs, 10 of which also set ceilings on check-cashing fees. Illi-

---

[11]Data from the Illinois Department of Financial Institutions show that check-cashing firms earn about 67 percent of their revenue from check-cashing fees and about 11 percent from sales of money orders. An Ernst & Young study commissioned by the Check Cashers' Association of New York reported similar percentages for New York CCOs (Ernst & Young 1992). Finally, ACE America's Cash Express, Inc., a chain with about 200 CCOs located mostly in Texas, reported in a 1992 stock-offering prospectus that its outlets earn over 80 percent of their revenue from check-cashing fees.

[12]In his study of check cashing in New York City, Wolf remarks disapprovingly that, prior to the introduction of regulations forbidding it, some check cashers ". . . cashed postdated checks and charged a 'fee' for each day the check was not negotiated. Some did not even bother with the guise of the postdated check and made outright usurious loans" (Wolf 1975, pp. 21–22).

nois and New York were the first to establish such regulations, enacting legislation in 1943 and 1944, respectively. Delaware and New Jersey began to regulate CCOs in the 1950s. In the past 3 years, California, Connecticut, Georgia, Minnesota, Ohio, Rhode Island, and Washington have also introduced regulations.[13] The state regulations require CCOs to be licensed. They generally require check cashers to post their fees in a prominent location in the outlet and to provide customers with a receipt. Often, the regulations require the owner of a CCO to meet a minimum bonding or capital requirement, and they specify CCO record-keeping requirements. Typically, the state banking department is responsible for issuing licenses and enforcing the regulations. In addition, federal regulations require all enterprises, including CCOs, to report unusually large sales of money orders or high-value wire transfers. This is to prevent these means from being used for money laundering.

Table 3.4 shows the legal ceilings on check-cashing fees in the ten states that set such ceilings as of early 1993. Within a state, the maximum permissible fee sometimes varies, depending on whether the check is drawn on an in-state or an out-of-state bank or is a government entitlement, payroll, or personal check. The different ceilings on fees across categories reflect the different speeds with which checks clear, different default risks, and the desire to limit the fees that public aid recipients pay for cashing their entitlement checks. In some of the states, the ceiling rates are above the competitive market rates and are rarely binding.

In 1989 the Consumer Federation of America (1989) conducted a survey of the fees levied at 60 check-cashing outlets in 20 major cities across the United States. The outlets were located in states with binding fee ceilings and those without. The survey found that fees charged for cashing local payroll checks ranged from 0.9 percent of the face value of the check to 3.0 percent, with the majority of rates falling in the range of 1.0 to 2.5 percent.[14] The average rate was 1.74 percent. For government assistance checks,

---

[13] Wisconsin has long required check cashers to be licensed, but otherwise the state does not regulate check cashers' activities. A number of other state legislatures are considering introducing legislation.

[14] The 0.9 percent rate was presumably found in New York City, where that was the maximum permissible charge until late 1992.

Table 3.4 / Maximum Check-Cashing Fees in Regulated States: As of End 1992 (rates are a percentage of the face value of the check)

State	Legal Ceiling Rate
California	3.0 percent for government and payroll checks (3.5 percent without specified identification) or $3.00, whichever is greater. Permits one-time $10 fee to issue identification. Ceiling fees set in 1992.
Connecticut	2.0 percent for nonpublic aid checks and 1.0 percent for state public aid checks. Ceiling fees set in 1990.
Delaware	1.0 percent or $4.00, whichever is greater. This ceiling fee was set in 1989. The previous ceiling rate was 0.5 percent or $0.25, whichever was greater.
Georgia	The larger of $5.00 or 3 percent for public aid checks, 10 percent for personal checks, and 5 percent for all other checks (payroll). Ceiling fees set in 1990.
Illinois	1.2 percent plus $0.90. This ceiling fee was set in 1986. The previous ceiling rate was 1.1 percent plus $0.75.
Minnesota	2.5 percent for public aid checks above $500 (5 percent for a first-time customer), no limit on personal checks but the rate must be filed with the state Commerce Department and be "reasonable," 3.0 percent on all other checks (6 percent for a first-time customer). Ceiling fees set in 1991.
New Jersey	1.0 percent for in-state checks and 1.5 percent for out-of-state checks or $0.50, whichever is greater. These ceiling fees were set in 1979. The previous ceiling rates were 0.75 percent on in-state checks and 1.0 percent on out-of-state checks, or $0.35.
New York	1.1 percent or $0.60, whichever is greater. This ceiling fee was set in November 1992. The previous ceiling was 0.9 percent, which was raised from 0.75 percent in 1988.
Ohio	3.0 percent for government checks. This ceiling became effective on January 1, 1993.
Rhode Island	Same as Georgia. Ceiling set in July 1992.

SOURCE: State regulatory agencies.

the rate ranged from 0.9 to 3.25 percent of the face value of the check, with an average rate of 1.73 percent. About a third of the check-cashing outlets contacted by the CFA were willing to cash personal checks. Not surprisingly, given the default risk, they charged far more for this service. In the survey group, fees ranged from 1.66 percent to 20 percent of the face value of the check and averaged 7.7 percent.

Average check-cashing fees in the states without binding ceilings tend to be somewhat higher than the averages found in the CFA survey. In my 1991 telephone survey of 42 check-cashing firms in several states, most CCOs in the unregulated states charged between 1.5 and 3.0 percent to cash government and local payroll checks.[15] The most common fee was 2.0 percent. Three outlets charged rates as high as 5–6 percent. Those that accepted personal checks charged 4–15 percent. A small number of the CCOs made payday loans, cashing personal checks postdated up to two weeks from the actual transaction. CCOs offering this service charged 20–35 percent of the face value of the check.

CCOs tend to set relatively low fees for money orders. The CFA survey found that the average charge for a $50 money order was $0.55, and many CCOs charged a flat fee independent of the size of the money order. This compares favorably with the $0.75 charged by the U.S. postal system for money orders up to $700. As explained by Jerome Gagerman (1990, pp. 3–4), the 1990 Chairman of the National Check Cashers Association, check cashers seek to promote money order sales because a check casher selling numerous money orders will not need to use as much of his own capital or tap a relatively expensive bank credit line to obtain cash for check-cashing customers. The check casher simply hands out the cash he receives from selling the money orders. In addition, check cashers can earn float (i.e., interest on money being transferred to someone else) from money order sales, for the check casher normally has a period of time before he must pay the company that provides the money orders.

---

[15] A telephone survey is, of course, not the ideal approach. One check casher, for example, told me: "A few sleazeballs in the business charge customers different fees, depending on what they think they can get away with. Anyone who is savvy enough to ask for the rate in advance would be charged less by these guys."

Comparing the Cost of Check-Cashing Outlets to Banks

Using the data on average fees for CCO services, one can easily estimate the cost to a household of meeting its payment needs through a CCO. To be conservative, consider the cost for a family that consistently cashes its paychecks or government entitlement checks at a check-cashing outlet charging a 1.75 percent fee and which buys four money orders a month at an average price of $0.50 per money order. Under these assumptions, a family with $10,000 in yearly take-home pay (about 75 percent of the 1990 official poverty level for a family of four) would spend $199 annually on basic financial transactions. A family with a $16,500 annual income (about 125 percent of the 1990 poverty level for a family of four) would spend $313 annually on basic financial services, and a family with a $24,000 income would spend $444 annually.

It is not possible to replicate exactly the cost of obtaining the same services from a bank, where "bank" is used generically to include commercial banks, savings banks, and savings and loans. This is because banks offer somewhat different services and impose different costs on their customers. Nevertheless, one can make a roughly accurate estimate on the basis of the data in the Federal Reserve Board's 1992 survey of bank fees and services (Board of Governors 1992). Based on the Board's data, the average annual cost of a single-fee, non-interest-bearing checking account with a balance of under $300 on which 6 checks a month were written was about $60 in 1991, assuming no checks were bounced. If checks were bounced, the cost of the account would have escalated rapidly, since the average fee for a bounced check was $15. If more than $400 were always maintained in such an account, the cost of the account would have fallen to zero since most banks waived account fees in this case.[16] If a depositor had forgone the option of writing checks and was able to keep at least $100 to $200 in a savings account at all times, the depositor also would have paid no fees at most banks. As is evident from these estimates, a family could lower substantially its expenditures for basic pay-

---

[16] The depositor would have paid no explicit fee for such an account, but would have paid an implicit fee because there was no interest received on the savings. This implicit fee would have amounted to about $15 over the year.

ment services by conducting its financial transactions through a bank rather than through a CCO, assuming that it does not bounce numerous checks.

One explanation for the vitality of the check-cashing industry in the face of this cost disadvantage is that out-of-pocket expenses do not measure the full cost of using a financial institution. Convenience and quality of service also matter. In these aspects, CCOs may have an advantage for many consumers since most CCOs have much longer opening hours than do banks, are located more conveniently for many consumers, and can be faster with the simple transactions in which they specialize.

A second explanation for the growth of CCOs in the face of banks' cost advantage is that bank services do not fully substitute for CCO services. Most importantly, while CCOs are willing to assume the risk that a check they cash will bounce, banks are not. Banks in urban areas generally refuse to cash checks drawn on other banks for nondepositors, even government checks with negligible default risk.[17] Banks will cash checks for depositors, but most banks require the customer either to maintain sufficient funds in an account to cover the check or to wait a few days for the check to clear. If a check the bank cashes bounces and the customer's account contains sufficient funds to cover it, the account is docked for the amount of the check. Many banks also charge the customer a fee for handling a "returned" deposit.

The Growth and Size of the Check-Cashing Industry

In interviews, check cashers who have been in the business many years said that the industry grew slowly until the early

---

[17] In 1988 the Consumer Federation of America (1988) surveyed 194 deposit institutions located primarily in the urban areas of 15 states and the District of Columbia. It found that out of the 191 institutions responding to the survey, 71 percent would not cash government checks for nondepositors at any price. Fourteen percent would cash nondepositors' government checks at no charge, and 15 percent would do so for a fee, averaging $3.88 for a $300 check. Outside of urban areas, banks are apparently more willing to cash government checks for nondepositors. A survey by the U.S. GAO suggests that banks that refuse to cash government checks for free for nondepositors do so because banks incur costs in handling checks, they do not want to crowd their lobbies with government aid recipients seeking only to cash entitlement checks, and they fear that some fraudulent checks might be cashed for which the government would not reimburse them (U.S. GAO 1988, pp. 13–17).

1980s. After that, it began to grow rapidly. Unfortunately, sufficiently longtime series of data are not available to confirm this.

Data are available for Illinois, New Jersey, and New York, but the trends in these states were probably influenced by unique factors. For example, in both Illinois and New York there was a sharp increase in the average annual growth rate in the number of licensed check-cashing outlets in the second half of the 1980s as compared to the first half of the decade. However, both of these states in the second half of the 1980s raised the ceiling on the fees that check cashers were allowed to charge. Moreover, New York, at the end of 1985, stopped considering distance between competing check-cashing locations as a factor in approving applications for licenses (Renshaw 1991, p. 8). In New Jersey the number of licensed check-cashing outlets grew strongly throughout the 1980s, rising from 69 in 1980 to 88 in 1989. However, the growth in the early part of the decade may have been aided by a 1979 increase in the fee that check cashers in New Jersey could charge. Finally, the trends in these states are unlikely to be nationally representative because Illinois, New Jersey, and New York, unlike other states, have had well-developed check-cashing industries for over 40 years. In fact, the study by Reeb et al. (1991) concludes that check cashing in New York City is a mature industry with limited future growth possibilities for its core services.

According to the information provided by American Business Information (ABI), there were 4,843 telephone book yellow-page listings of check-cashing (or currency exchange) outlets nationally in early 1992 (Figure 3.4). In late 1986, the earliest period for which it provided data, ABI reported just 2,151 national listings. These listings are probably roughly accurate, lower-bound estimates of the total number of CCOs in existence. In 6 of the 8 states that require CCOs to be licensed, for example, the yellow-page count closely approximates the number of licenses outstanding. However, the yellow-page count understated the number of licensed outlets in New York by about 20 percent and by almost 100 percent in Georgia. In any case, the evidence indicates that the industry has more than doubled in size in just 5 years.

Available data also show that the recent growth in CCOs has been uneven across geographic regions, with especially rapid growth outside of the few major urban areas where CCOs have

Figure 3.4 / Yellow-Page Listings of Check-Cashing Outlets:
1987–1992

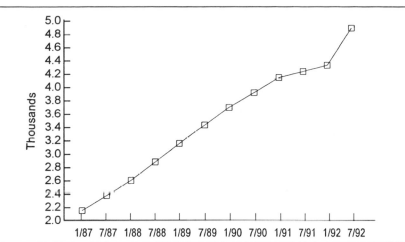

SOURCE: American Business Information Inc.

long existed. For example, yellow-page listings between late 1988
and early 1992 indicate that the number of CCOs in Illinois and
New York grew by 11 and 22 percent, respectively. Over that
same period of time, the number of listed check cashers grew by
110 percent in Florida, 265 percent in Georgia, 114 percent in
Maryland, 500 percent in North Carolina, and 124 percent in
Texas. In states with early and well-developed check-cashing
industries, recent growth has mainly occurred outside of the traditional center-city areas. For example, the Illinois Department of
Financial Institutions (1989, p. 5) reported that between 1985 and
1989, 108 new check-cashing licenses were granted, only 13 of
which were for locations in Chicago. Seventy-five of the new li
censes were for locations in the suburbs of Chicago, and the remaining 20 were for downstate locations.

CCOs are still largely concentrated in states with major urban
populations. Telephone listings from late 1991, for example, show
there were 1,089 in California, 706 in Illinois, 560 in Texas, 420 in
New York, 343 in Florida, 221 in Pennsylvania, and 98 in Ohio.
Within states, CCOs are disproportionately located in urban centers. A review of the 1990 addresses of CCOs in 8 states reveals
that fewer than 10 percent were located in cities of less than

100,000. The Illinois Department of Financial Institutions (1985, p. 107) reported that out of the 624 licensed check cashers in the state in 1985, 90 percent were located in the Chicago area. The concentration of CCOs in urban areas is not surprising; if a firm is to specialize in cashing checks for a fee, it must process a high volume of checks to cover personnel, property, insurance, and other expenses.

Given the sparse information on the check-cashing industry, any estimate of the size of the industry in dollar terms is subject to a large margin of error. However, a conservative estimate indicates that the industry cashed about 128 million checks in 1990 with a combined face value of $38 billion. From this activity, the check-cashing industry would have earned approximately $700 million in fees.

These estimates assume that there were 4,250 check-cashing outlets operating in 1990 and that they each cashed an average of 30,000 checks a year, or about 100 on a typical day. This estimate of the average number of checks cashed is below the scale of operation of most check-cashing outlets in Illinois, New Jersey, and New York, as reported by the regulatory agencies in those states. However, check cashers in other states told me that outlets in these 3 states must do a greater volume of business than the national average to survive because these states have binding ceilings on check-cashing fees. Check cashers in the unregulated states generally thought that most outlets handle between 20,000 and 40,000 checks annually. The estimates also assume that the average check had a face value of $300, and that the average cashing fee was 1.75 percent. The $300 estimate is consistent with the 1990 data for Illinois, New Jersey, and New York and was thought reasonable by check cashers in the unregulated states. The 1.75 percent fee is consistent with the estimated national average reported by the Consumer Federation of America (1989).

The Structure and Urban Location of the Check-Cashing Industry

In most areas, commercial check cashing is a highly competitive business, and barriers to entry into the industry are low. In the few states that require licenses, the registration process is generally rapid and open to almost anyone able to pay a modest fee. Other costs associated with opening a CCO are also within reach of many individuals. For example, in its initial stock offering prospectus, ACE America's Cash Express, a company with over 200 CCOs, reported that its capital cost for establishing a new outlet averaged $45,000 in 1992. Check cashing is also competitive because CCOs compete not only among themselves but also with grocery stores, bars, and other retail stores. To stimulate sales, some of these nonfinancial businesses cash peoples' checks at no charge or on condition that the customer make a purchase.

People in the check-cashing industry report that the majority of CCOs across the country are owned by local independent operators, many of whom own 3–10 outlets in a given area. However, large national chains are beginning to develop. At least 6 chains operated 50 or more outlets in 1991. Two of these, ACE America's Cash Express and the Pay-O-Matic Corporation, own over a hundred outlets each, and their stock is publicly traded in the over-the-counter market. There are also check-cashing franchise operations that have grown rapidly in the past few years. Recently, Western Union, which provides money-wiring services to many check cashers, has begun to develop a national network of check-cashing outlets (*Wall Street Journal* 8/23/91).

As with pawnshops, in recent years CCOs have been moving out of their traditional concentration in poor urban neighborhoods and into lower-middle-class suburbs, generally along heavily traveled roads. They are, nevertheless, still disproportionately located in lower-income areas. Kemlage and Renshaw relate that the New York State Banking Department found that 69 percent of all CCOs in New York City in 1990 were located in low-income census tracts. Robert Avery, in a study of the location of financial institutions in 5 major cities, found that in 1989 there were 0.08 CCOs per 10,000 inhabitants in zip code districts with an average household income of above $30,000. In zip code districts with an average household income of below $20,000, there were 0.73 CCOs per 10,000 inhabitants. Avery also found that CCOs were disproportionately represented in districts with high concentrations of African American residents.

A PORTRAIT OF FRINGE BANKERS

Since there are thousands of pawnbrokers and check cashers, any generalization will have many exceptions. Moreover, my impressions are largely shaped by the pawnbrokers and check cashers who met with me and who spoke openly about their businesses. These fringe bankers, most of whom were active in their professional associations, tended to be more successful in the business, were more concerned about maintaining professional ethical standards, and had a longer-term commitment to the business than did those who were reluctant to speak with me.

The most accurate, brief description of pawnbrokers is that they are somewhat typical small-business people. They generally own their own shops; most work long hours in the business; and many work alongside their spouses or other family members. The typical broker is probably around 50 years old, and many have retired from other professions. For example, the owner of the Hock It To Doc stores in Los Angeles is a retired dentist. Brokers who inherited their pawnshops from their parents tend to be younger than average. Almost all of the brokers that I met completed high school and many had college educations. Most used personal computers effectively in their businesses and actively followed new developments in the industry. Most pawnbrokers are men, but several of the more prominent in the profession, including a recent president of the professional association, are women. I have never met an African American pawnbroker, and it is my impression that there are very few Asian American or Hispanic brokers. Otherwise, the ethnic characteristics of pawnbrokers reflect those of the regions in which they work. Many in the major cities in the Northeast are Jewish, especially those who have been in the business many years. In the South and Southwest, the vast majority probably have a Christian heritage.

Most pawnbrokers express fairly high job satisfaction—particularly valuing the independence that comes with self-employment. In fact, perhaps because much of the public looks on pawnbroking disapprovingly, the business attracts many people who consider themselves mild social renegades. Many brokers express a love for the profession and appreciate the truths and folklore about its history. Independent brokers worry about the rise of the chains and whether their stores will be able to survive the competition. When they complain, pawnbrokers commonly lament their long hours of work, the rudeness of some customers, and the difficulty of finding reliable, honest employees. Many also worry about the possibility of armed robberies.

Commercial check cashers share most of the traits of pawnbrokers. A larger percentage of check cashers live in large cities since CCOs are still heavily concentrated in urban areas. There is less professional pride in check cashing, perhaps because the industry does not enjoy the rich history associated with pawnbroking. Most check cashers told me that they like their work, but they all add that worries over the dangers associated with potential robberies detract from their job satisfaction. Perhaps even more than pawnbrokers, check cashers complain of difficulties in finding competent employees whom they can trust not to steal part of the cash they handle.

4 / Who Uses Fringe Banks and Why?

Borrowing from a pawnshop is much more expensive than borrowing from a bank, finance company, or drawing on the line of credit provided with a bank credit card. It is also generally less convenient because the customer must carry his or her collateral into the shop and leave it in the possession of the broker. Similarly, obtaining payment services from a check-cashing outlet is substantially more expensive than obtaining these services through a bank. These observations immediately raise the question: Who uses these fringe banks and why do they choose to do so? This chapter offers answers to these questions. To do so, it draws on a wide range of evidence, including customer surveys, personal observation and interviews, and corroborating indirect data.

PAWNSHOP CUSTOMERS

Unfortunately, there have been no formal surveys of pawnshop customers; a portrait of the customer base of the industry must be based on other information. However, interviews with pawnbrokers and some of their customers and time spent observing pawnshop activity provide a fairly clear picture of who is using pawnshops and their reasons for doing so. This picture is also consistent with the evidence from indirect statistical data.

In interviews, almost all pawnbrokers say that their loan customers come from a variety of socioeconomic groups, but that the vast majority of their customers have low or moderate incomes ($9,000–$17,000 per year) with a high school education or less. The typical customer is probably younger than average for the adult population: many are between 18 and 30 years old. A disproportionate percentage of customers is African American or Hispanic. Many customers change jobs frequently and spend periods out of the labor force. A typical customer might work as an enlisted person in the military, a nonunion factory worker, a nurse's aide, a retail sales clerk, or a general helper in an automobile service station. Pawnbrokers believe that most of their customers rent their homes and that many move frequently, have bad credit records, and do not maintain bank accounts. They believe that a large share of their customers generally live from paycheck to paycheck and do a poor job of managing their personal finances. The brokers guess that few of their customers have bank credit cards.

Although embellished by colorful phrasing, the portrait the pawnshop chain, Cash America, presented of its customers is typical of that provided by most pawnbrokers:

> [Our customers] do not use checking accounts or credit cards, but choose to pay bills and purchase goods and services with cash and money orders.

> . . . The cash-only individual makes up the backbone of America. He's the hard-working next door neighbor, the guy at the corner service station, or the lady who works as a checker at the local supermarket. [Cash America, Inc. *Annual Report* 1989, p. 4]

Pawnbrokers do not ask their customers what they plan to do with their loans, but many customers volunteer that information. Brokers say that the loans are commonly used for a wide range of activities, including paying rent, fixing a car, buying Christmas presents, buying alcohol, illegal drugs, or food, paying for a vacation, gambling and buying lottery tickets, paying medical bills, purchasing gasoline for the car, etc.

> Why do these people need a pawnshop? First, there are times when they need extra cash. Maybe a child is ill and the doctor's bill must be paid. Maybe the car needs a new transmission. There are countless reasons why the customer might have an emergency need for cash. [Cash America, Inc. *Annual Report* 1989, p. 4]

In 1990, the Provident Loan Society, the unique not-for-profit pawnshop in New York City, asked its loan customers to complete a brief survey on a voluntary and anonymous basis. In explaining their reason for borrowing, 53 percent of the customers checked "family or personal emergency," and 28 percent checked "pay or consolidate bills."

Pawnbrokers commonly criticize some of their customers' lack of financial self-discipline and believe that this contributes to their economic hardship. The president of a regional pawnbrokers' association described some of his customers to one journalist, saying:

> They needed food for the baby. They needed diapers. The power company was going to turn off the power, and then they spend half of what you give them before they leave the store. They see the boom box they have to have. They see the TV they have to have and they *have* to have it. [Shaughnessy 1993, p. C-2]

In interviews, pawnbrokers provided fairly consistent explanations for why their customers, when they do need to borrow, turn to pawnshops. Some do because they are excluded from bank or finance company loans. Others use pawnshops for their discretion and convenience—cash loans are disbursed in a matter of minutes with very few questions asked. Across the nation, however, almost all pawnbrokers say the overwhelming majority of their customers belong to the first group. They indicate that there is little chance that most of their customers would pass a credit-risk screening procedure to obtain a loan from a bank or finance company or to obtain an unsecured bank credit card. In fact, Jack Daugherty, the founder and CEO of Cash America, remarked to a journalist: "I could take my customers and put them on a bus and drive them down to a bank and the bank would laugh at them. That's why they're my customers."[1]

Interestingly, pawnbrokers also say that most of their customers pay little attention to the interest rate or other fees on the loan. Their concern is the amount that the broker will lend on the collateral. Consequently, brokers say that pawnshops compete among themselves more on the basis of which one will make the largest loan relative to the collateral than they do on the basis of interest rates. Brokers attribute such customer behavior to a necessity to raise a certain amount of cash to meet a particular expenditure and to careless intertemporal budgeting.

Personal observation, informal interviews with pawnshop customers, and available data suggest that these descriptions of customers are broadly accurate. For example, most pawnbrokers described their loan customers as people who keep their financial savings in cash and live largely from one paycheck to the next. As will be discussed in more detail in the next chapter, data from the Federal Reserve Board's 1989 Survey of Consumer Finances show that about 14 percent of all households with incomes below $84,000 (in 1991 prices) had neither a checking nor savings account with any type of deposit institution, 31 percent of households with incomes below $18,000 had no such accounts, and 41 percent of households with incomes below $12,000 had no deposit account.

Table 4.1 uses data from this survey to contrast the socioeconomic characteristics of households without deposit accounts to those with accounts. For technical reasons, the data in the table exclude families with more than $84,000 in income. As shown in the table, families without bank accounts tend to fit the general characteristics that pawnbrokers attribute to their customers. They have substantially lower income than those with accounts. The families are also less likely to be headed by someone who is married, employed, white, or male. Families without bank accounts

---

[1]Kleinfield 1989, p. 37. But most pawnbrokers are generally very careful about stating publicly that the majority of their customers have no alternative credit source. Although this observation emphasizes that pawnshops are needed, it can also be used against pawnbrokers to argue that they have significant market power relative to their customers.

Table 4.1 / Selected Characteristics of Households with and
without Deposit Accounts (mean values): 1989

	Has Account	Does Not Have Account
Number of Households	1,809	282
Income (1991 dollars)	$34,214	$12,738
Number children	0.67	1.0
Percentage homeowners	65.7	24.1
Characteristics of Heads of Household		
Age	51.0	45.5
Years education	12.6	9.9
Percentage married	62.2	34.4
Percentage employed	67.8	43.3
Percentage minority	18.2	60.6
Percentage male	74.0	51.4
Credit Card (cc) Holdings		
Percentage w/ bank cc	63.0	5.3
Percentage w/ general purpose cc	11.4	3.5
Percentage w/ store cc	67.1	12.0
Percentage w/ gas cc	29.3	2.5

SOURCE: Author's estimates based on the Federal Reserve Board's 1989 Survey of
Consumer Finances.

NOTES: The four types of credit cards are bank credit cards (such as VISA or Master
Card), general purpose credit cards (such as American Express and Carte Blanche),
gasoline credit cards, and store credit cards that can be used at only one store or chain
(such as department store credit cards).

are also less likely to own their home, tend to have more children
living at home, and are generally headed by someone younger
and less educated than families with accounts. While 63 percent
of households with deposit accounts had bank credit cards, only
5 percent of those without accounts did.

Pawnbrokers' descriptions of their customers and why they
borrow are also consistent with Alan Andreasen's (1975) empirical
study of lower-income households. Based on his own research
and that of others, Andreasen concluded that lower-income consumers are much more likely than the middle class to have low
financial savings and unstable incomes and employment patterns.

He found that this increased their need for credit to smooth consumption patterns and to handle emergencies. These same characteristics—low savings and unstable incomes—also made it less likely that such consumers could honor debt payment commitments reliably, explaining why many had bad credit records.

THE CUSTOMERS OF CHECK-CASHING OUTLETS

Commercial check cashers describe their customers in terms that are broadly similar to those used by pawnbrokers in characterizing their loan customers. CCO owners and managers say that their customers have mostly low or moderate incomes. However, the average CCO customer is probably somewhat more affluent than the average pawnshop customer, since CCOs have a larger share of discretionary customers who use CCOs for their speed and convenience. CCO operators suspect that many of their customers change jobs relatively frequently. They say that their customers generally have below-average education levels and are more likely to be young and nonwhite than the public at large. They also describe their customers as mainly living from paycheck to paycheck, although they commonly emphasize that a significant share of their customers have bank accounts. On the other hand, those without bank accounts tend to be the most regular customers of check-cashing outlets.

According to CCO owners, many customers use CCOs because they find the locations and business hours more convenient than those of banks. However, check cashers generally stress that, because most banks are unwilling to assume the risk of cashing a bounced check, they do not consider banks to be direct competitors for many of their customers. The check cashers suspect that a significant share of their customers with bank accounts do not have sufficient funds in the bank to cover the paychecks or government support checks that they seek to cash. Although these customers might save money by depositing the checks in their banks and waiting for them to clear, they prefer to pay a fee to have the cash instantly. Check cashers believe that this is because the customers are pressed to make some cash payments or they simply like having the cash in their hands quickly, even if it costs them more.[2] In addition, check cashers think that some of their customers simply feel more comfortable in check-cashing outlets than they do in banks.[3] Finally, check cashers acknowledge that some customers may use CCOs as part of avoidance schemes.

Check cashers' belief that many of their customers with bank accounts do not have enough money in their accounts to cover their paychecks is consistent with available data. As shown in Table 4.2, the 1989 median account balance for households with bank accounts and household incomes below $21,545 was $967 in 1991 prices, where this number combines all balances in a household's deposit accounts of whatever type. If households headed by those aged 60 and older are excluded, the median drops to $549. However, 25 percent of such households had less than $203 in their bank accounts. Among households earning less than $11,970 in 1991 prices and maintaining at least one bank account, those in the lowest 25 percent in terms of their combined account balances had $170 or less in the bank.

In addition to the informal descriptions of customers by commercial check cashers, there have been two formal surveys of CCO clients. Although neither survey can claim to cover a representative sample of CCO customers, together they provide a broadly accurate portrait.

In 1989 the Consumer Bankers Association (CBA) hired the Roper Organization to survey check-cashing customers in five cities. In the survey, the Roper Organization interviewed about 20 exiting customers per check-cashing outlet from 25 outlets located in five major urban areas (Washington, D.C., Chicago, Los Angeles, Miami, and New York City). The organization selected

---

[2] A CCO customer, who has the option to deposit her check in a bank and wait a few days for it to clear, but who chooses to discount the check at a CCO, pays a high implicit interest rate. For example, if the CCO charges a 2 percent fee and the check would have taken 3 days to clear through the banking system, the customer is effectively paying a 248 percent annual interest rate to obtain cash more quickly.

[3] Pawnbrokers are also aware that some of their customers are uncomfortable in more formal settings. In fact, when I attended the 1991 conference of the National Pawnbrokers' Association, one of the dinner table conversations concerned whether pawnbrokers ought to wear ties at work. The consensus among the brokers at the table seemed to be that they ought to dress more or less like their customers so that the customers would feel comfortable interacting with them. In the course of the conversation, one of the brokers related the following joke: "What's the difference between a pawnbroker and a banker? The banker wears a tie."

Table 4.2 / Median Balances in Families' Deposit Accounts: 1989 (savings and checking accounts combined)

	Median Account Balance	Bottom Quartile Account Balance
Family Income Less than $21,545 (in 1991 $)	967	330
And age of family head less than 60	549	203
Family Income Less than $11,970 (in 1991 $)	604	275
And age of family head less than 60	483	170

SOURCE: Author's estimates based on the Federal Reserve Board's 1989 *Survey of Consumer Finances.*

outlets located within six blocks of a bank branch and timed the interviews to coincide with common payday dates in the area.

The CBA survey found that 37 percent of check-cashing customers were between 18 and 30 years old, and 5 percent were over 60 years old. Seventy-three percent were employed full-time and 12 percent part-time. Sixteen percent reported less than a high school education, and 29 percent reported a household income of less than $15,000 a year. The median reported household income was $20,400 (the median household income nationally in 1989 was $30,468). Thirty-three percent of the respondents were white, 47 percent black, and 18 percent Hispanic.

The CBA survey asked check-cashing customers whether they had bank accounts, how often they used check-cashing services, and why they used these services. Sixty-seven percent of the customers reported that they had a deposit account of some type with a bank, savings and loan, or credit union. Of the respondents with deposit accounts, 13 percent reported that they always used a check-cashing outlet to cash their checks, while the rest reported occasional use. When asked why they were using a CCO, 80 percent of those with deposit accounts said that they found the CCO's hours more convenient, the CCO was faster, bank lines were too long, or the CCO's location was more convenient. Seventeen percent said that they needed their money immediately and that they could not or did not want to wait for the check to clear through a bank. The remaining 3 percent offered a variety of other explanations.

Those without deposit accounts were asked why they did not have accounts. Thirty-one percent said it was because they did not have enough money; 10 percent said that banks cheated them with too many service charges; and 8 percent said that they had just moved into new areas. A wide variety of other explanations were offered less commonly. The CCO customers were also asked, "As far as you know, would it cost you more to have a bank account than what you pay for a check cashing service . . . or would [it] cost you about the same?" Fifty-seven percent of the respondents thought that check-cashing services were more expensive, and 32 percent thought that banks were more expensive or did not know which was more expensive.

Finally, both those with and without deposit accounts were asked whether they agreed or disagreed with a number of statements. Fifty-four percent agreed that "Check cashing services are easier to deal with than banks." Sixteen percent agreed that "There is not a bank near where I live." Twenty-four percent agreed that "Banks are too cold and impersonal with people like me." Sixty-one percent agreed that "Check cashing services charge too much."

Although the CBA survey results are informative, one should not take them as representative of an unbiased sample of check-cashing customers. First, customers who visit a CCO during a heavy payroll period are certainly more likely to be employed, to maintain a deposit account, and to have higher education and income levels than the general customer base. Second, the CBA's decision to interview customers only at CCOs within 6 blocks of a bank branch could bias the results, since bank branches are less likely to be located in poor neighborhoods and areas with high concentrations of African American residents (see Chapter 5). Third, the time of day during which the interviews were conducted could also affect the findings. Customers interviewed outside of normal banking hours might use check-cashing services for different reasons than would those using them at midday. Finally, the Roper Organization did not report whether all the customers contacted agreed to an interview, so there could be a selection bias.

An alternative survey of CCO customers was conducted by the New Jersey Department of the Public Advocate in 1987. In its study, the Department sampled only CCO customers cashing public assistance and social security checks.[4] The New Jersey agency interviewed 750 recipients of government transfer payments as they exited from 29 check-cashing firms dispersed throughout the state. Fifty-seven percent of those surveyed were cashing AFDC checks, 11 percent were cashing social security checks, 9 percent were cashing supplemental security income checks, and the rest were cashing unemployment benefit, veterans assistance, or state disability checks.

In the New Jersey survey, 92 percent of those interviewed said that they did not have bank accounts. Seventy-nine percent of the CCO clients stated that they never go to a bank to cash their government checks and, of these, 61 percent said they go only to CCOs. When asked why they were using a CCO to cash their government checks, 50 percent responded that banks were less convenient, 20 percent that they did not have a bank account, 20 percent that banks refuse to cash their checks, and 7 percent that there were no banks nearby. Since only 8 percent of the respondents had bank accounts, many of those without accounts attributed their decision to use a CCO to other considerations.

By interviewing only recipients of government support checks in one state, this survey clearly did not cover a representative sample of CCO customers nationally. Just as those interviewed in the survey by the Consumer Bankers Association would have been more affluent and more likely to be employed than the average CCO customer, the sample in the New Jersey study would have exhibited a bias in the opposite direction. This is reflected in the statistics on the ownership of deposit accounts; 67 percent of the respondents in the CBA survey had accounts while only 8

[4] New Jersey Department of the Public Advocate. "Who's Checking?" January 1988. Appendixes P–S indicate that CCOs in 3 New Jersey counties (Camden, Essex, and Mercer) cashed about 1.5 million checks in 1986, about 13 percent of which were AFDC checks. By examining 4,842 canceled AFDC checks from the 3 counties, the Department found that 47 percent of them were cashed at banks, 32 percent were cashed at CCOs, 12 percent were cashed at local businesses, and 9 percent were cashed by friends, relatives, or landlords. Of the AFDC checks cashed at banks, 75 percent were cashed at banks that serve as depositories of county funds and which are required to cash AFDC checks for nondepositors without a fee.

percent of those in the New Jersey survey did. The true percentage for CCO customers nationally would lie between these extremes. In any case, a judicious weighting of the results in both surveys provides a portrait of CCO customers that broadly agrees with that provided by CCO owners.

ECONOMIC JUDGMENT
AND THE DISCRETIONARY USE OF FRINGE BANKS

These portraits of fringe bank customers indicate that many people use pawnshops or CCOs because they have no reasonable alternatives. Some pawnshop customers may be reluctant to borrow at a 200 percent annual interest rate, and yet they must obtain money to pay the rent or to repair a car to get to work. If they also have bad credit records or no banking history, pawnshops may be their only source for loans. Similarly, some CCO customers may wish that they did not have to pay $6 to cash a $300 paycheck. Yet those without access to sufficient funds in a bank account who are facing an urgent need to pay bills may feel that they have little choice.

The evidence also indicates that many people use fringe banks on a discretionary basis. In the case of pawnshops, most customers probably have few credit alternatives, or they would not pay such high fees for loans. Many, however, are discretionary customers in the sense that they borrow to finance expenditures that are not necessities or for expenditures that might have easily been delayed until the next paycheck. Similarly, many CCO customers with bank accounts could deposit their checks and wait 3–5 days for them to clear. They consider, however, the instant access to cash offered by a CCO or its more convenient location and operating hours worth the additional expenditure.

Even some customers who use fringe banks out of necessity could be discretionary users from another perspective. Although they might have no short-run alternatives to fringe banks, this situation could be a result of earlier choices. A customer who, for example, squanders his paycheck on nonnecessities may need to turn to a pawnshop later in the month to help pay the rent. Or a customer who never makes any effort to save out of her paycheck may need to use a check-cashing outlet because her local banks will not cash checks drawn on other banks for nondepositors.

Although it is evident that there are large groups of discretionary and nondiscretionary fringe banking customers, it is not possible to be more precise about the relative shares of the customer base made up by these two groups. Existing surveys cannot answer this issue, and it would be difficult to design a survey that did. For example, without financial histories, it would be hard to know whether a customer was forced to use a pawnshop due to bad luck or to an indulgent lifestyle. No survey is likely to uncover detailed financial histories for a large sample of representative customers. Even if it were attempted, survey respondents might be unwilling to reveal unfavorable information about themselves. We must therefore be satisfied with the less precise conclusion pointed to by available evidence: a significant share of fringe banking customers are discretionary customers.

In view of the high cost of fringe banking services, one wonders why any consumers, especially those with modest incomes, would use them on a discretionary basis. The earlier discussion points to four explanations. First, in the case of CCOs, some customers may not be aware that CCO payment services are more expensive than comparable bank services. As noted above, the Consumer Bankers Association survey of CCO customers without bank accounts found that 32 percent either thought that bank accounts were more expensive than CCO services or did not know which was more expensive.

Second, the surveys of CCO customers also suggest that many customers, who are aware of the higher direct cost of CCO services and could or do maintain bank accounts, cash their checks at CCOs because they value a CCO's convenient location or hours of operation. In some cases, selecting a CCO for convenience could be economically motivated, since transportation or other costs could make mainstream financial institutions more expensive than the CCO.

The third explanation for the discretionary use of both pawnshops and CCOs is that they permit customers to shift expenditures forward in time. In the case of pawnshops, the loan enables a discretionary customer to make a nonessential expenditure immediately. In exchange, the customer must lower future expenditures, since the principal and interest on the loan must be repaid at a later date to redeem the collateral. If the collateral is not redeemed, the loan lowers the customer's future wealth. Many pawnshop customers willingly make this trade-off of future for current consumption. CCOs also provide instant cash when they discount customers' checks, allowing the customers to make discretionary expenditures immediately rather than waiting for checks to clear through the banking system. If the customers were to wait for their checks to clear, they would obtain the full face value of each check rather than a discounted value. Thus, as with pawnshops, the discretionary CCO customer makes an intertemporal trade-off. A substantial share of customers use CCOs specifically for this service.

Studies in other markets also find that some people are willing to pay a substantial premium in order to obtain a desired service or good instantly. For example, Swagler and Wheeler (1989) investigated why customers, who are mostly lower-income, patronize rent-to-own stores. These stores permit a customer to rent consumer durables, such as television sets, with ownership acquired at the end of the rental period, commonly 78 weeks or 18 months. Swagler and Wheeler found that the cost of acquiring a television set through such rental-purchase agreements is 2–2½ times more expensive than an outright purchase would be. Based on their own survey of a selected sample of 61 rent-to-own customers, the authors concluded that the main reason people entered such rental-purchase agreements were: (1) they want to obtain the good right away rather than delay while they accumulate savings; (2) they do not need to pass a credit-screening check at the rent-to-own stores; and (3) people like the low periodic payments and the flexibility of discontinuing the contract at any time by returning the rented good to the store.

In another example, the *Wall Street Journal* (3/20/91) reported that H & R Block's tax preparation customers who paid $20 or more in 1991 to have their returns filed electronically could also pay an additional $30 to obtain a "refund-anticipation" loan. With this loan, the filer obtained a tax refund 14 days earlier than the normal allotted time. Given that the average refund was $916 for the 1990 tax year, the typical H & R Block customer who chose this option was effectively paying an annual interest rate of 85 percent on the loan. According to H & R Block, the "overwhelming majority" of electronic filers sought the loan.

The willingness of many people to pay a relatively high percentage of the amount advanced in order to obtain cash for immediate discretionary expenditures is consistent with recent research in economics and psychology. Loewenstein and Thaler (1989) report the results of several experiments conducted by different researchers designed to discover the discount rate that people apply to monetary and nonmonetary events. They found three common conclusions in these experiments. First, if one compares the annualized discount rate people are willing to pay to receive a sum of money immediately rather than 3 days later to the rate that they are willing to pay to receive the sum immediately rather than 1 year later, the former is much higher than the latter. Second, the larger the sum of money people expect to receive at a future date, the smaller the discount rate they are willing to pay to advance the payment date. This suggests that people focus on the absolute amount of money they must pay to speed up a payment, rather than the percentage rate they pay. Third, people are willing to pay higher discount rates to advance the date of a payment than they are willing to pay to delay the date of a loss.

These findings can help explain the discretionary use of CCOs and pawnshops. In fringe banking transactions the customers pay a small absolute amount of money, but a relatively large percentage of the reward, to obtain the reward (cash) immediately. Since all three experimental findings are evident here—the length of time to be waited is short, the reward is relatively small, and the reward is positive—one would expect customers to be willing to pay a very high implicit or explicit interest rate, and they do.

The fourth explanation for the discretionary use of fringe banks is closely related to the third but, because it is couched in broader, normative terms, it is more socially sensitive. It holds that some people use fringe banks because they have made little effort to save out of their incomes, either because they placed almost no value on accumulating savings or they had too little self-discipline to do so. Such individuals, who have no financial savings, may be forced to use fringe banks for basic financial services.

No one claims that profligate behavior is confined to low- and moderate-income households, but social scientists have given far more attention to improvident consumer decisions by lower-income households than to shortsighted behavior by the more affluent. Undoubtedly, this focus is explained by two considerations. First, because shortsighted behavior is costly, it is likely to impose a much greater hardship on those with low incomes. Second, there is a widespread presumption that improvident spending is more common among lower-income households and households headed by individuals with less education. In fact, some social scientists have argued that lifestyle choices are responsible for much of the hardship associated with low household incomes. Edward Banfield, for example, wrote that much of American poverty ". . . is inwardly caused, and improvements in external circumstances are likely to affect it gradually if at all. Poverty of this type tends to be self-perpetuating. . . . In principle, it is possible to eliminate the poverty (material lack) of such a family, but only at great expense, since the capacity of the radically improvident to waste money is almost unlimited" (1974, p. 143).

Despite the widespread notion that lower-income households tend to be more shortsighted and wasteful in their spending behavior, this has not been demonstrated in statistical studies (Loewenstein 1992, pp. 23–24). Rather, most of the evidence for the proposition consists of anecdotes. Nevertheless, many social scientists accept it as true and have offered various theories to explain the phenomenon. For example, some commentators have viewed "improvident" behavior by lower-income families as caused by a moral failure or inadequate self-discipline. Those who hold this view, while not denying that there are many causes of poverty, attribute a significant share of the responsibility for economic hardship to the families themselves. A second theory attributes any shortsighted consumer orientation of low-income families to inherited cultural values. Social scientists in this tradition do not blame the poor for their situation because they argue that the cultural values that trap them in poverty were acquired from the family or community in childhood. The behavior is not a moral failure or a reflection of inadequate self-discipline, but the failure of society to teach better values. A third theory attributes observed improvident behavior among lower-income households to outside economic and social conditions. It stresses that if the poor tend not to plan for the future, it is because, ". . . their futures are bleak and they lack the resources and opportunities for doing much about it" (Steinberg 1981, p. 125). According to this view, the pressures of dealing with everyday economic crises create a present-time oriented behavior. If lower-income families are more profligate or shortsighted than other families, this does not explain their economic situation. Rather, the behavior is largely a natural response to the economic situation itself.

Although it is useful to classify these views, a balanced account would recognize that all three can be correct. One can demand responsibility from individuals for their actions while acknowledging that factors over which the individual has no control also shape behavior. It is also important to be realistic about the economic significance of spending and budgeting errors by low-income families. Staffers at not-for-profit agencies specializing in credit and budget counseling for low-income families have told me in informal interviews that budgeting mistakes are responsible for only a small part of their clients' economic problems. In their experience, the level and instability of their clients' incomes were far more important factors.

Several counselors also said that many of their clients' bad credit records were largely attributable to government-guaranteed student loans that they had taken out to attend trade schools. These schools led the clients to believe that upon graduation they could find employment as beauticians, truck drivers, electrical appliance repair specialists, etc. After completing the courses, however, the clients were not able to find employment in these fields, or were hired in menial jobs at wages far below those indicated by the schools' salespeople and subsequently fell behind in servicing their student loans.

5 / Explaining the Boom in Fringe Banking

The boom in pawnshops and check-cashing outlets began in the late 1970s and gathered momentum in the 1980s. I believe that one of the more important factors contributing to this growth was a marked increase in the number of households without bank accounts. These households were largely excluded from the payment and credit services of mainstream financial institutions. The increase in households without bank accounts was in turn mainly the result of a variety of socioeconomic and regulatory changes that reduced the ability of many households to save and increased the cost of maintaining deposit accounts with small balances.

Other factors also contributed to the fringe banking boom, some of which affected the demand for fringe banking services and some of which affected the supply. These include an increase in households' credit risk; a reduction in unsecured, nonrevolving consumer lending by banks and small loan companies; increased immigration; an increase in gold prices; a spreading awareness among entrepreneurs of the business opportunities in fringe banking; and a growing preference among consumers for instant services.

THE DECLINE IN THE OWNERSHIP
OF DEPOSIT ACCOUNTS

The most comprehensive data sources documenting the decline in the ownership of bank accounts over the 1980s are the 1977 Consumer Credit Survey and the 1989 Survey of Consumer Finances, which were conducted by the Survey Research Center at the University of Michigan with the sponsorship of the Federal Reserve Board and other government agencies. Both surveys asked about 2,500–3,000 families detailed questions about their socioeconomic characteristics, including their assets and liabilities. The families were selected to obtain nationally representative samples. In the survey, families were defined to include the head of household—normally the individual holding the title or lease on the housing unit—and all other persons living in the dwelling unit related to the head of household. Under this definition, a family might consist of a single individual.

Because the two surveys treated wealthy families differently, to make the surveys comparable I examine only the responses of families with less than $83,780 in income, calculated in 1991 prices.[1] This is equal to $35,000 in 1976 prices, which was a cut-off category in the 1977 survey. Since fewer than 10 percent of U.S. families in 1991 had incomes above $80,000, and certainly more than 98 percent of these families had bank accounts, the truncation of the data sets should not limit the analysis. After eliminating families with incomes above $83,780 in 1991 prices and dropping observations with missing responses, the 1977 data set contained responses from 2,025 families, and the 1989 data set contained responses from 2,091 families.

Table 5.1 examines changes in the percentages of households in the surveys with bank accounts, broken down by household socioeconomic categories.[2] In the table and the discussion that follows, the term "bank account" is used in its generic sense and

---

[1] Caskey and Peterson (1994) has a detailed discussion of the surveys and a more complete analysis of the data and trends.

[2] Because the surveys attempted to obtain nationally representative samples, the percentages of households without bank accounts in the samples should reflect the percentages nationally. There are, however, several potential reasons why the correspondence may not hold exactly, including inaccurate survey responses, nonresponses to particular questions, refusals to participate in the survey, and sampling errors.

Table 5.1 / Percentages of Households with Deposit Accounts of any Type

	1977	1989
All Households	90.5	86.5*
Income (in 1991 $)		
Up to $11,969	70.3	59.2*
$11,970–$21,545	86.2	85.8
$21,546–$29,925	93.7	92.5
$29,926–$47,875	95.9	97.2
$47,876–$83,780	99.6	98.3*
Age		
Less than 25 years	88.6	70.7*
25–64 years	91.4	85.6*
65 years and older	87.8	91.8
Education		
0–8 grades	76.9	69.8*
9–11 grades	83.9	77.2*
High school	94.1	85.8*
Some college	97.1	94.3*
College degree	99.0	98.4
Race		
Minority	71.6	65.8*
White	93.6	93.0

SOURCE: Caskey and Peterson (1994) based on the Federal Reserve Board's 1977 and 1989 *Survey of Consumer Finances.*

*The hypothesis that the percentage in the category stayed the same or increased from 1977 to 1989 can be rejected at a 5 percent significance level.

includes checking or savings-type accounts at banks, savings and loans, savings banks, and credit unions. Dollar amounts in the tables and the discussion below are in 1991 prices, unless specifically stated otherwise. In addition, in the tables, a "minority" head of household includes African Americans, Native Americans, Asians, Pacific Islanders, and Hispanics.

Among all families with less than $83,780 in income, the percentage without bank accounts of any type rose from 9.5 percent in 1977 to 13.5 percent in 1989.[3] This increase was not, however,

---

[3]The U.S. GAO (1988) conducted a study of bank account ownership using 1985 Bureau of the Census data. It found that about 17 percent of U.S. families did not

evenly distributed across socioeconomic categories. Among some groups, such as families headed by individuals 65 years old and older, the percentage of families without bank accounts declined, and the percentages for other groups stayed roughly constant. However, for families with less than $11,970 in income, about 20 percent of the population, the percentage of families without bank accounts rose from 30 percent in 1977 to 41 percent in 1989. Statistically significant increases were also found among households headed by individuals younger than age 65, households headed by individuals with less than 4 years of college education, and by households headed by racial or ethnic minorities.

This increase (from 9.5 percent in 1977 to 13.5 percent in 1989) in households without bank accounts implies that the number of households nationally without bank accounts rose from about 6.5 million in 1977 to about 11.5 million in 1989. The evidence in earlier chapters on who uses fringe banks and why they choose to do so indicates that these 11.5 million households would be prime candidates to be fringe banking customers. Undoubtedly, the near doubling in the number of households without deposit accounts between 1977 and 1989 increased the demand for fringe banking services and contributed substantially to the growth in pawnshops and CCOs.

This analysis leads one to wonder what caused such a large increase in households without bank accounts. Three possible causes are analyzed: an increase in fees on deposit accounts with small balances; the closing of bank branches in lower-income neighborhoods; and a broad range of socioeconomic changes that led to an increase in the percentage of households without financial savings, living largely from paycheck to paycheck.

Increases in Fees on Deposit Accounts with Small Balances

One prime suspect behind the decline in the ownership of bank accounts is the increase in fees during the 1980s on deposit accounts with small balances. In 1977, banks faced almost no compe-

---

have bank accounts. Some of the difference in their findings and ours may arise from the difference in the way a family is defined. In the GAO study, for example, single individuals do not constitute a family. Other differences may arise from differences in the years of the surveys and sample sizes.

tition from money market funds for deposits. Regulations set ceilings on the interest rates banks could pay on deposits, and restrictions on entry into banking limited other types of competition among banks. The low competitive pressures in this environment enabled banks to offer many services on which they lost money, making it up by paying below-market interest rates on large deposits. Among the money-losing services most banks offered was to permit depositors to maintain checking accounts with very small balances and low fees or no fees. With the deregulation of banking in the 1980s, banks were forced to pay market interest rates to attract large deposits. This in turn prompted them to eliminate money-losing services that they had previously offered. They commonly did so by introducing minimum balance requirements and raising fees on small accounts.

Even with the higher fees, maintaining a bank account and clearing one's paychecks through a bank would be significantly less costly than regularly using a check-cashing outlet. Some may conclude, therefore, that bank fee increases could not have prompted people to close their bank accounts. That conclusion would be erroneous: some people may have alternative sources, such as supermarkets, which cash local paychecks for free. Others may find the convenience of a CCO worth the additional cost, especially if their banks raised account fees and narrowed the cost differential.

The U.S. General Accounting Office (1987) conducted an extensive study of changes in deposit account fees between 1977 and 1985 at banks and savings and loans, also known as thrifts. In the study, the GAO surveyed 1,662 banks and thrift institutions between August 1985 and March 1986, requesting data on account fees and policies in 1977 and 1985. It had a 67 percent overall response rate, with fewer banks answering the questions concerning their 1977 policies. Based on these data and assumptions about the banking behavior of typical consumers, the GAO concluded that between 1977 and 1985 banks and thrifts increasingly charged account maintenance fees or required a minimum balance to avoid the fees. It found that consumers who paid fees to maintain non-interest-bearing checking accounts in 1977; i.e., mostly those with relatively small balances, generally paid from $22 to $37 annually in fees, in 1985 prices. By 1985, these consumers were generally paying from $41 to $57 annually to maintain such accounts.

Drawing on the GAO data and a recent report by the Board of Governors of the Federal Reserve System (1992), one can update the GAO report and add a few more details. Table 5.2 shows the evolution of fees on two types of non-interest-bearing checking accounts between 1977 and 1991. The data are for banks in the strictly defined sense; they do not cover thrift institutions or credit unions. In the table, all dollar amounts are quoted in 1991 prices to permit meaningful comparisons.

Between 1977 and 1991 the percentage of banks that offered non-interest-bearing checking accounts free of all fees fell from 35 percent to 5 percent. But the median minimum balance required to avoid paying fees fell from $675 in 1977 ($300 in 1977 prices) to $300–$400 in 1991. In 1977 the median monthly fee at banks that imposed only a flat monthly fee on the account was $2.24; in 1991 it was $5.00. The 1977 median monthly fee in banks that imposed both a flat fee and a per check charge was $2.24, and the median per check charge was $0.11. By 1991, these charges had risen to $4.00 and $0.25, respectively. The median fee for a bounced check

Table 5.2 / Changes in Bank Fees on Non-Interest-Bearing Checking Accounts (in 1991 $)

	1977*	1991*
Percentage of Banks Offering Accounts without Service Charges	35%	5%
Median Required Minimum Balance to Avoid Service Charges	$675	$300–$400
Median Monthly Charge on Fee-Only Accounts	$ 2.24	$ 5.00
Median Monthly Fee on Accounts with Fees and per Check Charge	$ 2.24	$ 4.00
Median per Check Charge	$ 0.11	$ 0.25
Median Fee for Writing Check with Insufficient Funds to Cover It	$ 11.25	$ 15.00

SOURCES: U.S. General Accounting Office (1987) and Board of Governors of the Federal Reserve System (1992).

*Data for 1977 are for banks and savings and loans. The data for 1991 are for banks only.

rose from about $11 in 1977 to $15 in 1991. Based on these data, the median annual cost in 1991 prices to maintain a non-interest-bearing checking account with a balance of under $300 on which 6 checks a month were written rose from between $27–$35 in 1977 to $60–$66 in 1991, assuming no checks were bounced.

Undoubtedly, in response to fee increases, some consumers with small bank accounts decided that it was no longer worthwhile to maintain bank accounts. In a professional magazine for savings banks, for example, a New Hampshire savings bank reported that it introduced in 1983 a $1 monthly fee on savings accounts with balances below $100 (Linnen 1983). Subsequently, the bank lost 24 percent of its deposit accounts, almost all of which were very small accounts. As a result, the banks' total deposits in dollars declined only 1.6 percent, and the average account balance rose from $1,875 to $2,414. The bank reported that the loss of these small accounts increased its profitability due to the cost of maintaining them. Many of the accounts that left the New Hampshire savings bank may have been transferred to other banks, but some undoubtedly left the banking system altogether.

Bank Branch Closings

A second factor that has been widely cited as contributing to the decline in the ownership of bank accounts is an apparent rash of bank branch closings in low-income and minority neighborhoods in the 1980s. Newspaper accounts over the past decade have told of bank branch closings that left some urban areas completely without bank representation.[4] If such closings were common, this could have led to an increase in the number of low-income and minority households not using banks for lack of convenient access. Others might keep a bank account but patronize a check-cashing outlet because of its more convenient location.

Unfortunately, there have been few empirical analyses of bank branch closing patterns. Those that do exist support the conclusion that in some large cities bank branch closings were disproportionately located in low-income and minority neighborhoods,

---

[4]For examples of the press attention given the subject, see the articles by Bartlett (1989), Gross (1987), Lueck (1988), and Zamba (1987).

leaving many of these urban areas completely without bank representation. In other urban areas, however, there is no evidence of such a trend and, in some cases, low-income and minority neighborhoods have more bank branches than do more affluent areas or neighborhoods with larger percentages of white residents.

Two studies have focused on bank branch closings in New York City. Margaret Stix (1986) studied the closings that took place between 1977 and 1984. In these 8 years, 130 bank branches closed, and Stix found a disproportionate number closed in low-income and minority areas. Stix also examined bank branch openings, finding most occurred in middle- and upper-income neighborhoods and in the suburban counties that ring New York City. A report by New York State Senator Franz Leichter (1989) examined commercial bank branch closings and openings in the New York metropolitan area from 1978 through 1988. The findings are similar to those of Stix: Bank closings disproportionately hit poor and minority areas of the city, and openings were concentrated in the more affluent suburbs.

More recently, Robert Avery (1991) conducted a multicity study of the location of banks and other financial institutions in 1977 and 1989 in five cities: Atlanta, Boston, Cleveland, Detroit, and Philadelphia. He found that zip code areas with relatively low median annual household income levels ($20,000 and below in 1989 prices) or with relatively high concentrations of black residents (50 percent or more) had fewer bank branches per capita in 1989 than did other areas.[5] Avery also examined the change in the number of banks and thrifts per capita between 1977 and 1989 across different zip code districts. Aggregating the cities, he found no evidence of a reduction in the number of banks per capita in the relatively low-income areas and only slight evidence in areas with large numbers of black residents. Unfortunately, he did not present information distinguishing these trends in the individual cities.

Taking an approach somewhat similar to that of Avery, I re-

[5]In his analysis, Avery emphasizes that much of the underrepresentation of banks in low-income and minority communities appears to be explained statistically by low housing values and the paucity of business activity in those areas. Establishing this correlation, of course, does not indicate the direction of causation.

cently conducted a study of trends in bank branch representation from 1970 through 1989 in five cities: Atlanta, Denver, New York City, San Jose, and Washington, D.C. My study differed from Avery's in several respects. I used census tracts, which contain on average about 4,000 residents. This smaller unit of analysis was appropriate for my study because I focused on changes in the number of communities completely without banks, while Avery studied changes in the number of banks per capita. Avery studied the location of banks, thrifts, check-cashing outlets, and loan and mortgage companies. My study included only F.D.I.C.-insured financial institutions.

A study of the distribution of banks across census tracts does not suggest that every census tract should have a local bank or that residents of census tracts without banks necessarily have less convenient access to banking services than do those in tracts with banks. It is possible that people in a tract without banks have ready access to banks just outside the tract's borders. Moreover, given that census tracts in densely populated areas of cities are sometimes only a few square blocks in size, a person in a tract without a bank may not have to travel far to find one. However, if there is a systematic underrepresentation of banks in census tracts with large percentages of low-income residents or racial and ethnic minorities, then there is a strong presumption that banks are generally less accessible to these communities than to others. This is especially true given that low-income tracts and tracts with large concentrations of minorities are often grouped in urban areas.[6]

Table 5.3 summarizes the principal results of the study. In the table, trends in bank branch locations are examined across five different categories of census tracts: tracts with a median household income below 67 percent of the citywide median and tracts with a median household income above this level; tracts with more than 50 percent African American residents or more than 40 percent Hispanic residents; and tracts with less than 50 percent African American and less than 40 percent Hispanic residents. The cut-off point for Hispanic communities differed from that for

[6]Ideally, one might use a map to calculate the average distance between specified communities and the nearest bank. My method is less costly and can, therefore, more readily be extended to multiple cities.

Table 5.3 / Changes in Bank Representation: 1970–1989

ATLANTA	1970	1980	1989
Total Number of Banks	78	92	100
Tracts with Median Household Incomes Below 67 Percent of City Average			
Percentage of tracts w/banks	19.4	19.4	13.9
Mean number of banks	0.28	0.33	0.25
Tracts with Median Household Income Above 67 Percent of Average			
Percentage of tracts w/banks	46.6	47.9	49.3
Mean number of banks	0.93	1.1	1.25
Tracts with More than 50 Percent African American Residents			
Percentage of tracts w/banks	29.2	26.4	23.6
Mean number of banks	0.38	0.42	0.36
Tracts with More than 40 Percent Hispanic Residents			
Percentage of tracts w/banks	NA	NA	NA
Mean number of banks	NA	NA	NA
Tracts with Less than 50 Percent African American and 40 Percent Hispanic Residents			
Percentage of tracts w/banks	54.1	62.2	64.9
Mean number of banks	1.38	1.68	2

NEW YORK CITY	1970	1980	1989
Total Number of Banks	805	1068	999
Tracts with Median Household Incomes Below 67 Percent of City Average			
Percentage of tracts w/banks	23.5	20.7	16.7
Mean number of banks	0.36	0.35	0.29
Tracts with Median Household Income Above 67 Percent of Average			
Percentage of tracts w/banks	23.7	29.9	28.1
Mean number of banks	0.43	0.61	0.58
Tracts with More than 50 Percent African American Residents			
Percentage of tracts w/banks	16.8	16.4	12.7
Mean number of banks	0.25	0.22	0.17
Tracts with More than 40 Percent Hispanic Residents			
Percentage of tracts w/banks	25.4	22.9	19.9
Mean number of banks	0.4	0.42	0.37
Tracts with Less than 50 Percent African American and 40 Percent Hispanic Residents			
Percentage of tracts w/banks	20	32.4	30.7
Mean number of banks	0.47	0.68	0.65

Table 5.3 / (*continued*)

	DENVER		
	1970	1980	1989
Total Number of Banks	39	42	70
Tracts with Median Household Incomes Below 67 Percent of City Average			
Percentage of tracts w/banks	26.9	23.1	30.8
Mean number of banks	0.85	0.73	1.15
Tracts with Median Household Income Above 67 Percent of Average			
Percentage of tracts w/banks	13.4	19.6	30.9
Mean number of banks	0.18	0.24	0.41
Tracts with More than 50 Percent African American Residents			
Percentage of tracts w/banks	10	10	10
Mean number of banks	0.1	0.1	0.1
Tracts with More than 40 Percent Hispanic Residents			
Percentage of tracts w/banks	14.3	14.3	19
Mean number of banks	0.14	0.14	0.24
Tracts with Less than 50 Percent African American and 40 Percent Hispanic Residents			
Percentage of tracts w/banks	17.4	22.8	35.9
Mean number of banks	0.38	0.41	0.7

	SAN JOSE		
	1970	1980	1989
Total Number of Banks	47	94	99
Tracts with Median Household Incomes Below 67 Percent of City Average			
Percentage of tracts w/banks	33.3	52.3	42.9
Mean number of banks	0.81	1.48	1.67
Tracts with Median Household Income Above 67 Percent of Average			
Percentage of tracts w/banks	24.1	38	35.2
Mean number of banks	0.28	0.58	0.59
Tracts with More than 50 Percent African American Residents			
Percentage of tracts w/banks	NA	NA	NA
Mean number of banks	NA	NA	NA
Tracts with More than 40 Percent Hispanic Residents			
Percentage of tracts w/banks	27.6	41.3	27.6
Mean number of banks	0.41	0.9	0.97
Tracts with Less than 50 Percent African American and 40 Percent Hispanic Residents			
Percentage of tracts w/banks	25	40	39
Mean number of banks	0.35	0.68	0.71

Table 5.3 / *(continued)*

WASHINGTON, D.C.			
	1970	1980	1989
Total Number of Banks	78	107	138
Tracts with Median Household Incomes			
Below 67 Percent of City Average			
Percentage of tracts w/banks	17.2	20.7	31
Mean number of banks	0.72	0.69	1
Tracts with Median Household Income Above 67 Percent of Average			
Percentage of tracts w/banks	26.4	34.3	37.1
Mean number of banks	0.41	0.62	0.78
Tracts with More than 50 Percent African American Residents			
Percentage of tracts w/banks	18.7	22	26
Mean number of banks	0.2	0.24	0.28
Tracts with More than 40 Percent Hispanic Residents			
Percentage of tracts w/banks	NA	NA	NA
Mean number of banks	NA	NA	NA
Tracts with Less than 50 Percent African American			
and 40 Percent Hispanic Residents			
Percentage of tracts w/banks	41.3	58.7	63
Mean number of banks	1.15	1.7	2.24

SOURCE: Caskey (1994).

African American communities because there were very few tracts with 50 percent or more Hispanic residents. The socioeconomic characteristics of the census tracts were specified using the 1980 census data. At the time the study was undertaken, the 1990 census data were not available. Moreover, in examining the change in bank representation from 1970 to 1989, the socioeconomic characteristics of the tracts at the 1980 midpoint is appropriate.

Before discussing the trends in the table, it is interesting to examine the cross-sectional representation of banks as of 1989. In Atlanta and New York City, the relatively low-income census tracts were significantly less likely to have a local bank than were the more affluent tracts. In addition, the mean number of banks per tract in the lower-income tracts was substantially below that of the more affluent tracts. This pattern does not hold, however, in the other cities. In Denver, San Jose, and Washington, there is no statistically significant difference between the likelihood of a bank existing in one of the lower-income tracts compared to the other tracts, and in these cities the mean number of banks per tract in the lower-income tracts is higher than that of the more affluent tracts.

Cross-sectional patterns based on the racial or ethnic composition of the tracts are more consistent than those based on income. In all of the cities except San Jose, which had no tracts with 50 percent or more African Americans, tracts with a majority of black residents were significantly less likely to have a local bank than were the nonminority tracts.[7] Moreover, the mean number of banks per tract in the tracts with a dominant percentage of black residents was significantly below that of the nonminority tracts. In fact, in all cases the percentage of tracts with banks or the mean number of banks per tract in the tracts with a majority of African Americans was less than half that of the nonminority tracts.

Patterns with respect to tracts with large concentrations of Hispanic residents are less dramatic. In Denver and New York City, census tracts with 40 percent or more Hispanic residents were significantly less likely to have a bank than were the nonminority tracts, and they had a lower mean number of banks per tract. However, in neither case was the difference between bank representation in the Hispanic communities and the nonminority communities as large as that between the African American communities and the nonminority communities. In San Jose, tracts with a large share of Hispanic residents had a lower percentage of tracts with banks than did the nonminority tracts, but the difference was not statistically significant. In addition, the mean number of banks per tract was higher in the tracts with a large share of Hispanic residents than in the other tracts.

The underrepresentation of bank branches in minority and some low-income urban communities may explain much of the demand for fringe banking services in these communities, but such patterns would have had to become significantly more pronounced over the past decade or two to increase the demand for such services. In this respect, the data are less supportive. The

[7] In my "Bank Representation in Low-Income and Minority Urban Communities" (1994), cross-sectional regression analysis indicated that, after controlling for city-specific effects and differences in populations and incomes across census tracts, tracts with higher percentages of African American or Hispanic residents in 1989 were less likely to have banks.

data from Atlanta and New York City are consistent with the hypothesis that banks disproportionately closed branches in lower-income communities, especially after 1980. But the data from Denver, San Jose, and Washington do not support the hypothesis. In these cities, the trend for the lower-income tracts is roughly parallel to that for the more affluent tracts. Similarly, in Atlanta and New York City, the tracts with high concentrations of minority residents show a decline in bank representation over the two decades, which stands in clear contrast to the increase in the nonminority tracts. In the other cities, however, the trend for the minority tracts generally differs little from that for the nonminority tracts.

These findings indicate that in some urban areas bank branch closings probably increased the demand for fringe banking services. In other cities, this is unlikely to have been a significant factor. More research is needed before definitive statements can be made about national trends. However, two observations suggest that bank closings are unlikely to explain national trends in bank account ownership or the demand for fringe banking services. First, the number of bank branches nationally grew over the 1980s. In 1980, there were about 57,000 bank branches or main offices across the country; by 1990, there were almost 67,000. Second, much of the growth in fringe banking occurred outside of traditional urban areas, where bank branch closings have apparently been concentrated.

Broad Socioeconomic Changes

Socioeconomic changes in the 1980s that reduced the ability of households to maintain savings were other likely influences on the ownership of bank accounts and the demand for fringe banking services. The stagnation or decline in the real incomes of many households in the lower end of the income distribution were especially important in this regard. As shown in Table 5.4, in inflation-adjusted terms the mean income for households in the lowest 20 percent of the income distribution rose by 24 percent between 1967 and 1978.[8] Between 1979 and 1991 it fell by 1.5 percent. Even

[8]The U.S. Bureau of the Census data on household and family incomes are drawn from a series of surveys which do not track particular households or families over

Table 5.4 / Mean Household and Family Income, by Quintiles: 1967–1991 (in 1991 $)

	Lowest Fifth	Second Fifth	Third Fifth	Fourth Fifth	Highest Fifth
		Households			
1991	7,263	18,149	30,147	45,957	88,130
1990	7,498	18,789	31,034	46,790	90,804
1989	7,682	19,113	31,771	48,058	93,944
1988	7,443	18,786	31,420	47,496	90,676
1987	7,352	18,684	31,238	47,218	89,797
1986	7,175	18,458	30,887	46,530	88,071
1985	7,106	18,009	29,892	44,964	83,990
1984	7,126	17,749	29,413	44,287	81,433
1983	6,910	17,357	28,698	43,064	79,066
1982	6,824	17,269	28,585	42,513	77,972
1981	6,957	17,330	28,708	42,793	76,441
1980	7,133	17,752	29,294	43,157	76,949
1979	7,373	18,339	30,236	44,372	79,631
1978	7,436	18,261	30,152	44,169	78,857
1967	6,003	16,633	26,557	37,157	67,335

at the 1989 peak of the 1980s business cycle expansion, the real mean income for households in the lowest quintile of the income distribution had risen only by 4.2 percent above its 1979 level, which stands in sharp contrast to the 24 percent gain of the 1967–1978 period. Trends for households in the second lowest quintile of the income distribution are broadly similar.

The trends for mean family income are parallel. Under the definition of the U.S. Bureau of the Census, the mean family income differs from the mean household income since it excludes the incomes of individuals living alone or with other unrelated individuals. The inflation-adjusted mean family income for families in the lowest quintile of the income distribution fell by 9.6

---

time. Thus, while the mean income of households in the lowest quintile of the income distribution grew by 24 percent from 1967 to 1979, this does not imply that the mean income of the particular families in the lowest quintile in 1967 grew by 24 percent over this period.

	Lowest Fifth	Second Fifth	Third Fifth	Fourth Fifth	Highest Fifth
			Families		
1991	9,734	23,105	35,851	51,997	95,530
1990	10,247	23,900	36,808	52,935	98,377
1989	10,359	24,184	37,571	54,055	101,780
1988	10,197	23,848	37,111	53,298	97,792
1987	10,157	23,872	37,069	53,053	96,956
1986	9,990	23,501	36,471	52,115	94,926
1985	9,675	22,711	35,132	50,356	90,627
1984	9,547	22,413	34,658	49,563	87,341
1983	9,236	21,823	33,648	47,964	84,381
1982	9,256	21,785	33,370	47,332	83,371
1981	9,782	22,126	33,958	47,682	81,741
1980	10,199	22,904	34,695	48,140	82,433
1979	10,765	23,750	35,870	49,395	85,589
1978	10,599	23,588	35,499	48,911	84,099
1967	9,106	20,606	29,619	39,723	70,141

SOURCE: *Money Income of Households, Families, and Persons in the United States: 1991.* Series P-60, No. 180, U.S. Department of Commerce, Bureau of the Census.

percent from 1979 to 1991, after growing by 18 percent between 1967 and 1979. In fact, even at the peak of the 1980s expansion, the real mean income of families in the lowest quintile of the income distribution never equaled its 1979 level. The real mean income of families in the second lowest quintile increased by 15 percent between 1967 and 1979. Between 1979 and 1989, it increased only by 1.8 percent, before falling in the 1990–1991 recession.

Along with the decline and stagnation in incomes of lower-paid households, there was a marked increase in the number of people falling below the officially defined poverty level between the mid-1970s and late 1980s. As shown in Figure 5.1, from 1959 through 1969, the number of people in poverty fell dramatically. From 1970 through 1978, this number fluctuated slightly around a fairly constant base. Beginning in 1979, however, the number of people

Figure 5.1 / Poverty Trends: 1959–1992

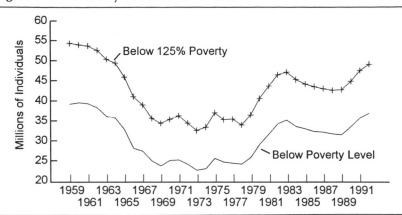

SOURCE: U.S. Bureau of the Census.

in poverty escalated rapidly, and declined modestly during the 1983–1989 expansion before turning upward again. Current research indicates that several socioeconomic developments account for the 1979–1992 increase in poverty, including technological changes that reduced the demand for low-skilled labor; increasing numbers of single-parent households with children; the decline of unions; greater reliance on imports for manufactured goods; and reductions in funding for income support programs (Danziger and Gottschalk 1993).

Whatever the causes behind the 1980s decline and stagnation in incomes of low-wage workers and the rise in poverty, one would expect these developments to reduce the savings of millions of households. Unfortunately, for purposes of comparison, satisfactory data on household savings are not available prior to 1983. However, the data that do exist support the supposition. In 1983 the Federal Reserve Board's *Survey of Consumer Finances* found that, among families with incomes of $10,000 or less (in 1989 prices), the median household net worth was $3,800 (Kennickell and Shack-Marquez 1992). In the 1989 survey, this had declined to $2,300. This change is particularly striking when one considers that 1983 was the trough of a serious recession and 1989 was the peak of a business cycle. The survey data also show that, while the median net worth of all families in the United States increased from $43,000 in 1983 (in 1989 prices) to $47,000 in 1989, the median net worth of minority families fell from $6,900 in 1983 to $4,000 in 1989.

As the incomes and wealth of millions of families in the lower end of the income distribution fell over the 1980s, many of them may have concluded that they no longer needed banks' saving services, and they closed their deposit accounts. Consequently, even if there had been no change in government regulations and bank policies, one would have expected a decline in account ownership because an increasing number of households were living from one paycheck to the next. For the vast majority of families, the first financial asset that they acquire is a deposit account. Thus, the decline in account ownership signaled an increase in the number of Americans without any financial savings of note.

In a recent statistical study, Peterson and I concluded that the socioeconomic changes that reduced the ability of millions of households to save were probably the most important factors behind the decline in account ownership. We used the 1977 data from the Federal Reserve Board's *Survey of Consumer Finances* to construct a probit model of the statistical correlation between the socioeconomic characteristics of households and the likelihood of their owning deposit accounts. Table 5.5 presents the results from the probit regression. In the regression, the dependent variable is a one if the household has a bank account and a zero if it does not. The results show that, controlling for the other variables, the likelihood that a family owns a bank account is positively related to the family's income and the education and age of its household head. Families that own their own homes and in which the household heads are employed and white are also more likely to have a bank account. This likelihood is also negatively related to the number of children in the household.

Although different interpretations of these results are possible, it is likely that these non-income variables are good predictors of account ownership because they are linked to a household's average income over a period of several years. Earnings fluctuate from year to year, as people work overtime, lose jobs, switch jobs, and the like. Thus, one would expect account ownership to be related not only to a household's income in the year of the survey but also to its average income over several years prior to the survey, since this would affect the family's ability to accumulate and main-

Table 5.5 / Probit Regression Study of 1977 Account Ownership (dependent variable is ownership of a deposit account)

Constant	−1.06	(3.3)
Income	0.030	(6.9)
Number of Children	−0.131	(3.6)
Age	0.006	(1.7)
Education	0.121	(7.4)
Married	0.127	(0.8)
Male	−0.078	(0.5)
Minority	−0.750	(6.8)
Employed	0.186	(1.6)
Homeowner	0.520	(4.7)

Log-Likelihood: −430.7
Chi-Squared Statistic (H_0: slope of coeffs = 0): 408
Number of Observations: 2,025
Percentage of In-Sample Correct Predictions: 91
(t-statistics are in parentheses)

SOURCE: Caskey and Peterson (1994), using data from the Federal Reserve Board's 1977 *Survey of Consumer Finances*.

NOTES: Variable Definitions

Income:	Household income in thousands of 1991 dollars.
Number of children:	Number of dependent children in the household.
Age:	Age of the head of household.
Education:	Years of formal education of head of household.
Married:	A dummy variable with the value 1.0 if the head of household is living with a domestic partner.
Male:	A dummy variable with the value 1.0 if the head of household is a male.
Minority:	A dummy variable with the value 1.0 if the head of household identifies himself or herself as nonwhite.
Employed:	A dummy variable with the value of 1.0 if the head of household is employed.
Homeowner:	A dummy variable with the value of 1.0 if the household owns its home.

tain savings. Holding household income constant in the survey year, it is likely that families with less education and those headed by a racial minority or an unemployed individual have lower long-term earnings than other families. One would also expect households with lower long-term earnings to be more likely to rent their homes. The number of children in a family is linked to account ownership because it affects a family's ability to save out of its income.

In a second step, we used the coefficients from the regression, as well as the data on household socioeconomic characteristics in the 1989 survey, to predict which households in the 1989 survey would have bank accounts. This method allows us to estimate the impact of socioeconomic changes on account ownership, holding bank fees and branch locations constant.

Table 5.6 indicates the results of this procedure. A comparison of the predicted pattern of account ownership to the actual shows that changes in the socioeconomic conditions of the surveyed households alone can explain the decline in account ownership between 1977 and 1989. One should not interpret this statistical result literally to mean that increases in fees on small accounts, the spread of minimum balance requirements, or bank branch closings had no effect on account ownership, for there is always some uncertainty about the correct specification of a regression model and the estimated coefficients.[9] However, the result does indicate that, across most categories of the population, one would have expected a decrease in the percentage of the population using banks close to the observed magnitude simply on the basis of changes in the socioeconomic conditions of the households.

Table 5.7 presents additional evidence that a household's ability to save out of its income is a major determinant of whether or not it owns a bank account. The 1989 *Survey of Consumer Finances* asked people who did not have checking accounts to identify the most important reason from a list of potential reasons for why they did not have a checking account. Table 5.7 reports the results for households without deposit accounts of any type. The most common reason people gave was that they did not write enough checks to make maintaining an account worthwhile. Close behind in importance was the response, "Don't have enough money." In

---

[9]The probit model estimates the probability that a household will have a deposit account. In generating the 1989 predictions, Peterson and I assumed that all households with a probability above a certain level would have an account, where the threshold was set to predict correctly the percentage of households in 1977 with accounts. To obtain a rough indication of the forecast uncertainty arising from the uncertainty associated with the estimated coefficients, we generated a set of 1989 predictions by changing, one at a time, the 1977 probit coefficients one and two standard deviations from their estimated values. While the original coefficient estimates imply that 85.6 percent of households in 1989 would have had deposit accounts (Table 5.6), varying the coefficients by one standard deviation generates predictions ranging from 79.7 percent to 90.7 percent. Varying the coefficients by two standard deviations results in predicted levels of account ownership ranging from 71.8 percent to 94.3 percent.

Table 5.6 / Predicted and Actual Percentages of Households
with Deposit Accounts in 1989,
by Socioeconomic Categories
(households with incomes below $83,780 in 1991 $)

	Actual	Predicted
All Households	86.5	85.6
By Household Income (1991 $)		
Up to $11,969	59.2	54.7
$11,970–$21,545	85.8	85.0
$21,546–$29,925	92.5	90.5
$29,926–$47,875	97.2	98.4
$47,876–$83,780	98.3	99.6
By Age of Household Head		
Less than 25 years	70.7	69.6
25 to 64 years	85.6	86.5
65 years and older	91.8	85.8
By Educational Attainment of Household Head		
0–8 grades	69.8	65.9
9–11 grades	77.2	71.3
High school	85.8	86.1
Some college	94.3	97.1
College degree	98.4	97.7
By Race of Household Head		
Minority	65.8	67.2
White	93.0	95.5

SOURCE: Caskey and Peterson (1994), using data from the Federal Reserve Board's
1977 and 1989 *Survey of Consumer Finances.*

fact, among families with less than $12,000 in income and among
minority families, the response, "Don't have enough money,"
was slightly more common than "Don't write enough checks to
make it worthwhile." About 15 percent of the respondents said
that they do not maintain checking accounts because of bank fees
or minimum balance requirements. Thirteen percent said that they
were uncomfortable dealing with banks. Less than 2 percent said
that they did not keep checking accounts because of inconvenient
bank locations.

Care should be taken in interpreting these survey responses,
for it is impossible to know how the respondents interpreted

Table 5.7 / Survey of Households without Deposit Accounts

Distribution of responses in 1989 survey to the request: "Looking at this list, please tell me which is the most important reason (you don't/your family doesn't) have a checking account." Responses are for families without deposit accounts of any type.

Number of Respondents	282
Percentage of Respondents Answering:	
"Don't write enough checks to make it worthwhile."	31.6
"Don't have enough money."	27.0
"Do not like dealing with banks."	13.1
"Service charges are too high."	7.8
"Minimum balance is too high."	7.1
"Can't manage or balance a checking account."	5.3
"No bank has convenient hours or location."	1.1
Other	7.1

SOURCE: Caskey and Peterson (1994), based on the Federal Reserve Board's 1989 *Survey of Consumer Finances*.

NOTE: Totals may not add to 100 percent due to rounding.

the questions. For example, the answer, "Don't have enough money," could have meant to some respondents, "In view of the minimum balance requirements and fees on small accounts, I don't have enough money to make it worthwhile to own an account." The answer, "Don't write enough checks to make it worthwhile," could have a similar interpretation. Despite the uncertainty in interpreting the responses, the results provide additional support for the conclusion that socioeconomic changes that reduced households' financial wealth over the 1980s were likely to have been major factors behind the decline in the ownership of bank accounts.

The rapid expansion in private banking over the 1980s provides additional evidence that the increased segmentation of the financial system largely reflected shifts in the distribution of financial wealth. Families at both extremes of the wealth distribution had special financial needs that mainstream financial institutions were ill-equipped to meet.

Traditionally, private banks were banks owned by partners who shared unlimited liability in the event of losses. Today, however, the term has come to mean financial institutions, often subsidiaries or departments of commercial or investment banks, that provide a range of banking and investment services for wealthy individuals. In the United States, most private banks require potential clients to have at least $1 million in liquid assets and an income of over $250,000 a year.

In the 1980s, there was an explosive growth in the number of commercial and investment banks offering private banking services. Most analysts attribute this boom in private banking to the 1980s run-up in asset prices, which greatly increased the wealth of many upper-income households. For example:

> The explosion of personal wealth in the 1980s led banks to seek to fill a niche. It was discovered that the market for private banking services had grown beyond the traditional market of elderly people with inherited wealth. [*Financial Times,* October 22, 1991, p. 37]

The analogy to the fringe banking boom is obvious. In fact, one might label the private banks, "high-end fringe banks."

Overall, the evidence therefore suggests four conclusions. First, over the 1980s there was a marked decline in the use of banks among lower-income households and households headed by nonwhites, the young, and the less well educated. This decline spurred the demand for payment services unlinked to banks' deposit services and for consumer loans to people unable to pass the credit screening procedures of mainstream financial institutions. Second, the decline in account ownership mainly reflected a deterioration in the economic situation of households in the lower end of the income distribution. Over the 1980s, the incomes of millions of these households fell, reducing their ability to save and, therefore, their need for banks' deposit services. Third, the decline in account ownership was exacerbated by increases in fees on deposit accounts with small balances. Fourth, the closing of bank branches in some low-income and minority communities was probably an insignificant factor behind the decline in account ownership nationally. However, it could well have been a significant local factor in some urban communities.

OTHER FACTORS BEHIND THE FRINGE BANKING BOOM

In addition to the decline in the ownership of bank accounts, other factors probably also contributed to the boom in pawnshops and check-cashing outlets. For pawnshops, the rise in consumer credit risk caused by the decline in many households' financial margins of safety may have been particularly important. A rise in credit risk can exclude someone from mainstream credit markets. Banks, for example, will generally not provide unsecured credit cards to consumers whose debt payments to income ratio rises above a certain threshold. A bank will not simply raise interest rates for high-risk debtors and continue to supply them with credit, for higher interest rates might only increase the odds that the debtors will not be able to repay the loans. Consequently, credit applications that are judged by banks or other unsecured creditors to be above an acceptable risk threshold are turned down.

Over the 1980s, the credit risk of many families increased significantly, increasing the percentage of the population cut off from mainstream credit sources. Data from the 1983 and 1989 Surveys of Consumer Finances, for example, show that in 1983 families with less than $10,000 income in 1989 prices, falling in the highest third of the debt service to income distribution, devoted 32 percent of their incomes to servicing nonmortgage debt (Kennickell and Shack-Marquez 1992). By 1989, this ratio had risen to nearly 40 percent.

Another signal of high credit risk, which cuts across all income groups, is a history of personal bankruptcy. In response to a variety of factors, including changes in bankruptcy laws and attitudes toward bankruptcy, there was a large rise in personal bankruptcy filings over the 1980s (Figure 5.2). In 1982 there were 311,443 nonbusiness bankruptcies filed in U.S. district courts. In 1991 there were 811,206 such filings, a 160 percent increase. Those declaring bankruptcy, as well as the many more who did not file for bankruptcy but whose financial margins of safety deteriorated substantially, would have found it much more difficult to obtain unsecured consumer loans. Undoubtedly, some turned to pawnshops to meet their credit needs.

Figure 5.2 / Nonbusiness Bankruptcy Filings: 1975–1991

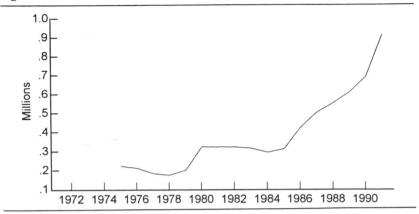

SOURCE: Administrative Office of the U.S. Courts.

A second element contributing to the expansion in pawnbroking was a contraction in the supply of nonrevolving, unsecured personal loans by banks and consumer finance companies. The development of the computer greatly lowered the cost of extending revolving lines of credit through bank credit cards. It did not bring similar cost reductions for one-time personal loans extended by bank loan officers and finance companies. In addition, changes in personal bankruptcy laws in 1979 increased the risk associated with unsecured loans. Consequently, banks and finance companies reduced the resources that they devoted to small, unsecured personal loans (Brown 1986, p. 56). Banks shifted toward credit cards and home equity loans. Consumer finance companies also emphasized home equity lending.

A third factor behind the fringe banking expansion was the increased immigration into the United States in the 1980s. From 1951 through 1980, the average annual immigration rate was about 1.8 legal immigrants per 1,000 U.S. residents. Over the 1980s, this rate was 3.1 legal immigrants per 1,000 residents (*1992 Statistical Abstract of the U.S.*, Table 5). There are no official estimates of illegal immigration, but it is widely thought that the expanding U.S. economy of the 1980s and the economic difficulties of many of the economies in the Caribbean and Central America spurred a significant increase in illegal immigration. A rise in either legal or illegal immigration could increase the demand for fringe banking services. Recent immigrants are likely to have less financial savings and a shorter history of verifiable employment, making them higher credit risks. Illegal immigrants without social security documentation are unlikely to be able to open bank accounts and, even if they could, many would probably fear that this might reveal their presence to immigration authorities.

A fourth factor contributing to the revival of pawnbroking was the increase in gold prices. In 1970 an ounce of gold sold for $36 ($128 in 1991 prices). Gold prices began to escalate rapidly after 1973, peaking in 1980 at $613 an ounce ($1,013 in 1991 prices). Over the 1980s gold prices receded, but always remained well above $300 an ounce in 1991 prices through the end of the decade. This increase in gold prices enabled pawnshops to make larger loans on jewelry. Because the transaction cost of making a loan is independent of the amount lent, this raised the profitability of many jewelry loans. It also might have added to the demand for pawnshop loans, as customers discovered that they could get larger loans on their gold jewelry.

A fifth factor behind the expansion of pawnshops and CCOs was a growing awareness among entrepreneurs of the business opportunities in fringe banking.[10] Awareness of the potential profits in the pawnbroking industry was fueled by the media attention given to the success of Cash America Investments. Because it was a novelty to have a pawnshop company traded on the New York Stock Exchange, and because the company's first few years were very successful, many newspapers and business magazines carried stories on Cash America. Until the end of the 1980s, news reports on check-cashing operations were less com-

---

[10]There is little support for the hypothesis that changes in states' pawnshop or CCO regulations created the 1980s boom. Georgia and North Carolina revised their pawnshop laws in 1989 and 1990 to make them much more favorable to the industry. In neither case, however, did this result in a big increase in the number of pawnshops. The muted reaction is not surprising since pawnshops in these states were generally charging much more than the legal maximum prior to the change. Illinois also revised its laws to permit pawnbrokers to charge higher fees, but this took effect only in 1991. Over the 1980s, other states made only small adjustments in their pawnshop laws, which did not materially affect the industry. In the case of CCOs, Delaware, Illinois, New Jersey, and New York slightly raised the fees that outlets could charge for cashing checks over the 1980s. Outside of these four states, however, regulations were not made more favorable to the industry.

mon. Nevertheless, as check cashers' bright business signs began to spring up at key transit points in urban areas across the country, public awareness of the business grew. This growing awareness fed the imagination of many entrepreneurs, some of whom entered the business *de novo*, others of whom decided to expand their existing operations into regional chains.

Finally, the growth of CCOs might have also been stimulated by a growing taste among the American public for instant service—and a willingness to pay for it. Such a demand shift might underlie, and be reinforced by, the expansion of fast-food restaurants, microwave dinners in the supermarket, instant photo finishing, express delivery services, and the like. As people became more accustomed to paying for rapid service, they increasingly turned to CCOs for rapid and convenient payment services.

6 / Regulating Fringe Banks

Pawnshop loans and CCO payment services are far more expensive than are credit or payment services from mainstream financial institutions. Yet millions of low- and moderate-income households rely on these fringe banks for basic financial services, and the number is growing. This raises the questions: Should a ceiling be placed on the fees that fringe banks can charge? How should fringe banks be regulated? Before addressing these questions, it is important to understand why fringe banking fees are so high.

WHY ARE PAWNSHOP AND CHECK-CASHING FEES SO HIGH?

When many people hear of the comparatively high fees levied by fringe banks, they assume that the owners of fringe banks must make a fortune at the expense of their customers. This reasoning, however, ignores the fact that both pawnbroking and check cashing are highly competitive businesses that are relatively easy to enter. No large-scale monopoly or cartel keeps fees above competitive levels. If a pawnbroker or check casher charges excessively high fees, another entrepreneur can compete by providing the same service at a lower price. One must therefore look to other reasons to explain the high fees in fringe banking. This section points to three principal causes. First, the cost of providing the credit or payment service is high relative to the size of the transaction. Second, fringe banks could lower their fixed costs per customer and their fees if they could operate at a larger scale, but transportation costs mean that customers are unwilling to travel far for small savings. Third, customers' transportation costs also give fringe banks some local monopoly power. In addition, the personal danger and stigma associated with operating a pawnshop or check-cashing outlet might increase fees.

Consider the process a bank follows in making consumer loans. The consumer completes a credit application that solicits a range of information to evaluate the consumer's credit risk. The bank checks this information and, depending on the indicated degree of credit risk, decides whether to extend the credit. To lower the costs of this procedure, banks provide approved consumers with a revolving line of credit in the form of a credit card and standardize application forms and approval standards. In this way, a computer can use the information provided by the consumer and a credit-rating agency to evaluate the consumer's credit risk and reject or accept the application. The computer can even write the letter notifying the applicant of the decision. Assuming that the application is approved, the computer will keep track of the credit outstanding on the card and send bills and record payments. A bank can extend one hundred small credit card loans to a consumer over a 10-year period, without the consumer ever personally speaking to a bank representative.

Now, consider the process a pawnshop follows in making a loan. For each loan, the client must bring the collateral to the shop. An experienced broker evaluates the collateral and offers to lend a specific amount based on the valuation. If an agreement is reached, the broker must complete a brief loan ticket and store the collateral during the period of the loan. If the loan is renewed, this is almost always done in person by the client. When the collateral is redeemed, that too requires the personal attention of a pawnshop employee. This same process is followed whether the customer is a first-time customer or has borrowed a hundred times from the shop. The process is labor-intensive, and the broker can use low-wage unskilled labor for only a part of it.

Based on this description, it is understandable that the fee on a $50 pawnshop loan must substantially exceed that on a $50 credit card advance. Since the typical loan for most brokers is less than $100, the fee that the broker must charge to cover the transaction cost will appear very high when expressed as an annualized interest rate. In fact, only a small part of this fee reflects the time value of money. Most of it reflects a broker's transaction costs. Since the pawnbroker's transaction costs associated with making a $25 loan do not differ substantially from that associated with making a $1,000 loan, brokers often charge lower interest rates on loans above a few hundred dollars.[1]

CCOs also face comparatively high costs per transaction, though less than pawnbrokers. To compete successfully, most CCOs are open 8–10 hours a day and some even longer, which results in long periods of idleness for attendants. Many CCOs are located in relatively high crime areas where business insurance is expensive. Each check that is cashed must be evaluated by an attendant who can distinguish high-risk from low-risk checks. Even very cautious check cashers occasionally cash bad checks, many of which they never collect on. For example, ACE America's Cash Express, the company operating a chain of over 200 CCOs, cashes only customers' payroll and government checks, a policy that lowers its odds of cashing a bad check. Nevertheless, its net bad check losses were 0.14 percent of the face value of the checks it cashed in 1992.[2] Check cashers must also pay for armored car

---

[1] In the 1920s and 1930s, several states passed laws limiting pawnshops to charging three percent a month in interest. At the time, this ceiling was not a major binding constraint for many brokers. Now, brokers in the states that have maintained 3 percent ceilings say that only brokers who do a very high volume of business can survive while observing this rate ceiling. The reason for this change is that productivity advances in the general economy have raised real wages substantially since the 1920s. Thus, even if the average value of the items pledged has stayed roughly constant in real terms over the past 70 years, labor costs relative to the value of the pledged items have risen, and the interest rate that brokers must charge to cover these costs has necessarily also risen.

[2] At ACE in 1992, the average face value of the checks it cashed was $276.35 (Prospectus for ACE America's Cash Express stock offering 12/2/92). Its average fee for cashing such a check was $6.33, or 2.29 percent of the average face value. Its average loss from bad checks was $0.38 per check, or 0.14 percent of the face value.

service and pay banks for cash advances and a range of payment services, including clearing a heavy volume of checks. All of these expenses must be covered in the check casher's fee.

Consumer transportation costs also affect the fees levied by pawnshops and CCOs. Fringe banks could lower their costs per transaction if they served more people, because the fixed costs of the businesses would be divided among more customers. Their customers, however, face nontrivial transportation costs traveling to and from pawnshops or CCOs. Because fringe bank transactions are quite small, customers tend to patronize the most conveniently located shops even if more distant shops charge slightly less for their services. Consequently, geographic areas are generally served by numerous, dispersed fringe banks, which operate at less than their most efficient scale. This raises the cost of fringe banking services but lowers consumers' transportation costs. On the other hand, when consumers select a bank credit card the physical location of the bank is of little importance. This allows banks to spread the fixed costs of a heavily computerized credit card operation among hundreds of thousands of accounts.

The high transportation costs relative to the size of the transaction in fringe banking also reduces competition in the industry: most pawnshops and CCOs compete only with other fringe banks located within a few miles of themselves.[3] In communities that are large enough to support only one pawnshop or CCO, a fringe bank could have a local monopoly. In other cases, a small number of fringe banks could explicitly or implicitly collude or locate strategically to keep out new entrants and keep fees above competitive levels. Such behavior could apply to any retail business where consumers pay transportation costs that are high relative to the size of the transaction. To the extent that it occurs in fringe banking, this too raises the price of fringe banking services.

Finally, even with relatively free entry into pawnbroking and check cashing, one would expect fringe banking to remain somewhat more profitable than other businesses requiring similar skills

---

[3]In the terminology of economics, pawnshops and check-cashing outlets, like many other retail businesses, are monopolistically competitive, with their products differentiated by location. In theoretical models intended to capture this characteristic, a wide range of economic results can be generated by varying the key assumptions of the models (Greenhut et al. 1987).

and capital. This is because the associated danger and stigma might discourage some entrepreneurs from entering it. Despite the efforts of many contemporary pawnbrokers to change the image of the business, there is still a popular perception that pawnbrokers operate dingy shops and prey upon the desperate poor. No matter how successful they might be, pawnbrokers are unlikely to be asked to join exclusive country clubs or civic organizations. In fact, one young broker, in lamenting the popular image of the business, explained to a journalist:

> It was a heavy thing when I was single and dating. "What do you do for a living?" "I'm a pawnbroker." It'd take a woman two hours to get over that. [Mano 1985, p. 59]

Check cashing does not have as well-entrenched a popular image, but in urban areas it too is often viewed as a disreputable business. Since most people use banks and do not pay explicit fees to cash their checks, they tend to think that anyone who charges mainly low- and moderate-income people for this service must be exploiting these customers.

There can also be relatively high personal risk in running a CCO or pawnshop. Many CCOs and pawnshops are located in high crime areas and both, especially CCOs, keep large amounts of cash on hand. Check cashers and pawnbrokers are constantly aware of the danger, which does detract from the appeal of the business. The woman who waited on me when I pawned a VCR at a pawnshop in Philadelphia wore a pistol in a shoulder holster to discourage robbers. When I attended the annual convention of the National Check Cashers Association, I asked numerous CCO owners if they enjoyed their work. Again and again, I was told, "Yes, but I don't like worrying about my physical safety or that of my employees." Some said that they drive to work using different routes and arrive at irregular times to reduce the chances that thieves would use them to gain entry to the outlet. Just as the wages of sanitation workers must compensate them for unpleasant aspects of their job, so too must the rate of return to pawnbrokers and check cashers compensate them for the social stigma and danger associated with their businesses.

Recognizing that fringe banks must levy relatively high fees

does not necessarily mean that public policy should be unconcerned about the fees currently charged by pawnshops and CCOs.
In addition, even if policymakers were to decide to leave the deter-
mination of these fees to the market, there are a number of other
issues concerning the behavior of fringe banks that they ought to
address. The next section discusses the regulation of pawnshops.
The final section discusses the regulation of check-cashing outlets.

REGULATING PAWNSHOPS

The pawnbroking industry, itself, is forcing many state legislators to take a new look at regulatory guidelines. As the number
of pawnshops has increased, so too has its political clout grown.
In many states with relatively restrictive usury laws, pawnbrokers
have organized to push for increases in interest rate ceilings or
other fees. Companies attempting to build national pawnshop
chains are keenly interested in these efforts, for their ability to
continue growing rapidly depends on the outcome. In the past
4 years, extensive lobbying from pawnbrokers has led Georgia,
Illinois, Indiana, Mississippi, and North Carolina to raise the fees
that pawnbrokers can levy on loans in these states.

Before discussing pawnshop usury laws, by which I mean any
limits on the fees pawnshops can charge, it is useful to examine
the general theoretical basis for treating pawnshops differently
from other retail businesses. The economic justification is parallel
to that given for the special regulation of banks, insurance companies, or securities markets (Goodhart 1989, pp. 206–213).[4] Retail
financial market transactions generally involve trust and information asymmetries to a degree unequaled in other retail markets,

[4] As a general rule, economic theory can support government regulation of markets
where there is market failure. Examples of market failure include barriers to entry into
an industry, limited availability of relevant information in a market, externalities, and
public goods. Whether the government should attempt to correct such market failures
through regulation depends on the economic significance of the market failures and
the cost-effectiveness of government regulations.

Economic theory maintains that concerns about the economic welfare of certain
social groups are best addressed by income transfers, not by price controls on the
goods these groups purchase. As a practical matter, however, governments often do
use market regulation to address distributional concerns. In some cases this is simply
poor public policy. In other cases, the government may be unable to identify the
people needing the transfers or could face other practical difficulties that make regulation, despite its problems, the best approach.

with the exception of professional services. Under these conditions, regulations can be a cost-effective way to reduce the risk to customers and to stimulate competition in the industry.

There is a substantial element of trust in pawnshop loan transactions. The customer must trust the broker to return the collateral in the same condition it was delivered. The customer also trusts the broker to take reasonable safeguards against fire or theft and to carry adequate insurance.[5] A retired New York City pawnbroker explained that not all brokers have merited this trust:

> As a matter of course any legitimate pawnbroker will note on his ticket stub the fact that a diamond is missing from a ring you just hocked or that your watch has been damaged in some way. But the sharper marks all his tickets, regardless of the collateral's condition, "stone out" or "stone missing" or "stone damaged." By so marking a ticket, the sharper can remove a stone and keep it with impunity—thus increasing his profit and acquiring a repair job as well. . . . Hock a set of tools with this kind of pawnbroker, and when you get the set back some of your tools will be missing. . . . While examining a piece of jewelry a dishonest pawnbroker will loosen a stone from a ring. . . . Once this is accomplished, he will point out to you that your diamond, ruby, sapphire, or emerald is missing. And it is only your word against his if you call the police. [Simpson et al. 1954, pp. 101–103]

If information flows among customers are good, competition should eventually drive such pawnbrokers out of business. However, since many customers are transient and some may feel ashamed about using a pawnshop, there are good grounds for believing that information about pawnshop behavior will not spread quickly in many communities.[6] Even when information spreads, it may not spread rapidly enough to prevent unscrupu-

---

[5]Brokers commonly maintain that they are not liable for losses arising from fire or theft. They argue that it is the owners' responsibility to cover the pledged collateral with homeowner's insurance.

[6]Customers' needs to trust that a pawnshop will take good care of their collateral might help to explain the recent success of pawnshop chains. If the chains build a reputation for honesty and reliability, pawnshop customers may patronize the chains rather than risk using an unknown pawnshop when they move or travel. If so, it is in the interest of independent pawnshops to set strict standards in the industry so that potential new customers will see little risk in patronizing an unknown independent.

lous brokers from victimizing numerous customers and hurting the business of honest brokers.

Because of brokers' fiduciary responsibility, it is understandable that most states have regulations denying pawnshop licenses to people with felony criminal records. It is also appropriate that states require brokers to be bonded and insured.

I advocate an additional measure. To speed the demise of unscrupulous brokers, states should require all brokers to post a toll-free consumer complaint telephone number and print this information on pawn tickets. Regulators could then single out for special scrutiny any broker against whom a disproportionate share of complaints are filed. If the complaints are judged to be justified and serious, the state should promptly remove the owner's pawnshop license.

As in other financial markets, asymmetries in financial sophistication are likely to be serious in pawnbroking. Pawnshop owners are generally considerably more sophisticated than their customers, many of whom would have difficulty calculating an interest rate. Moreover, many pawnshops have some local monopoly power arising from the significant consumer transportation costs relative to the size of the transaction. The information problems that pawnshop customers face and the potential market power of pawnshops justify several regulations, which most states already impose or partially impose. Setting minimum loan maturity standards and grace periods, for example, can limit the ability of brokers with market power to negotiate an unreasonably short loan period with customers. (Most states currently require brokers to hold pawned items for 2 months or more before selling them in order to give the police an opportunity to check for stolen merchandise.) Standardized maturity periods for pawnshops across a state can also enhance competition among pawnbrokers. By reducing the number of parameters that pawnbrokers can vary, consumers can more easily compare loan terms across shops.

Furthermore, state regulations should require pawnshops to post their loan fees prominently and in simple terms. Pawn tickets should also state fees in percentage terms as well as in dollar amounts appropriate for the size of the loan. Such measures, which many states already require, protect unsophisticated customers and spur competition among pawnshops. Competition can also be enhanced by setting limits on the number and types of fees that pawnshops can charge. It is easier, for example, for customers to compare fees when pawnshops are permitted to charge only a flat transaction fee and a monthly interest rate than when they can charge insurance fees, transaction fees, storage fees, and interest rates. Limiting the number of fees need not, of course, limit the amount pawnshops charge: it simply makes prices more transparent.

Although information problems or market power could be invoked to justify regulations requiring pawnshops to return any surplus from the sale of a forfeited pawn to the pledgor, such regulations do not work well in practice: they are easily evaded and their enforcement would require the expenditure of substantial resources. Moreover, the return of a customer's surplus often appears to be somewhat arbitrary, since many pawnshop customers move frequently without leaving forwarding addresses. Other customers do not provide a correct mailing address when pawning their items. Finally, if pawnshops consistently make good faith efforts to return any surplus, this adds to their costs and raises loan fees.

Concerns over some pawnshops' local market power can justify binding ceilings on pawnshop fees. Before a state sets such ceilings, however, it should explicitly recognize their effects. Economists have commonly noted that usury laws can be detrimental to low-income consumers because financial institutions under binding interest rate ceilings tend to allocate credit to only the most creditworthy borrowers, who generally belong to middle- and high-income groups (Nathan 1980). This is not the case for pawnshops. At pawnshops, all customers provide collateral, eliminating the need to distinguish high-risk from low-risk borrowers. The major effect of low ceilings on pawnshop loan fees is to reduce the number of pawnshops in a state.

A recent example illustrates this point. On July 1, 1992, Indiana raised the maximum monthly fee a pawnshop could charge on a $55 loan from $3.15 to $12.65. At the time it made the change, there were 35 pawnshops in the state. Five months later, there were 72.

A high pawnshop fee ceiling ensures the provision of convenient, very expensive, small collateralized credit to all. A low ceiling permits pawnshops to function profitably only in areas with high concentrations of potential pawnshop customers; i.e., largely urban areas, because with low fees only pawnshops with a very high volume of lending can cover their overhead.

Levine made this same point in 1911:

> . . . [P]awnbroking cannot be successfully carried on except in a large community having a densely crowded population. Even though the population be large enough, it is only when such communities have a thick congregated population of wage earners (such as is found in New York, Philadelphia, Boston, Chicago, and other of our principal cities . . .) that a pawnbroker doing business *legitimately* can exist on a low interest charge. [Levine 1911, p. 63] [italics mine]

In addition to the effect on the number of pawnshops per capita, pawnbrokers say that pawnshops make more small loans in states with high interest rates or fixed transaction fees. Although not enough state regulatory agencies report data to verify this claim, it is reasonable. In states with low interest rate ceilings, around 3 percent a month, it is not profitable to make loans of less than $25, and many pawnshops avoid doing so. Others violate the law by charging above the legal ceiling. Alternatively, one would expect the nonredemption rate to be higher in states where pawnshops are permitted to charge higher loan fees. This expectation is consistent with the data reported in Table 3.2.

States therefore face trade-offs in setting ceilings on pawnshop loans. Low ceilings benefit customers who live near surviving pawnshops and who pawn more valuable items. On the other hand, low ceilings can make pawnshops inaccessible to customers in less densely populated areas and to customers with only bulky low-value items to pawn. If customers' transportation costs are included in the calculations, low ceilings on fees could even raise the cost of pawnshop loans for customers who live far away from the surviving high-volume shops.

From a paternalistic viewpoint, some policy analysts might argue that ceilings on loan fees should be very low because the public is better off if pawnshops do not exist or are inconvenient. The rationale is that a ready availability of pawnshops encourages people to devote too large a share of their incomes for unnecessary credit expenses.[7] There is undoubtedly some truth in this. It is also true that people use pawnshops for purposes that almost everyone would approve of, such as borrowing money to fix a car to enable one to go to work.[8] Unfortunately, almost no information is available on small, secured loan arrangements in communities without pawnshops. However, in view of the potential for consumer abuse in credit markets, it is undoubtedly preferable to have a licensed and regulated pawnshop, rather than an unlicensed individual, provide small loans.

Based on these considerations, it is difficult to make a compelling case for stringent ceilings on pawnshop loan fees as long as the industry is competitive. Ceilings that are not too far from free market rates can be justified, however, since they reduce the probability that some unscrupulous brokers with market power would attempt to take advantage of the least sophisticated or most necessitous customers.

Economically sophisticated pawnbrokers are well aware that the way to raise their long-run profitability is to create barriers to entry into the business. In several states, pawnshop organizations have been lobbying to add clauses to state regulations that would prohibit new shops from opening within a certain distance of existing shops or that would require potential new owners to prove that they possess significant capital. In some states, these efforts have paid off. In Texas, for example, pawnbrokers recently lobbied for and attained a revision in the law whereby in order to open a new pawnshop the prospective owner must have net

---

[7]Mainstream economic theory assumes that consumers act so as to maximize their own well-being. Society often chooses to limit consumers' choices, however, out of concern that they will make shortsighted choices. For example, society forces all adults to save for retirement through social security contributions and limits customers' ability to buy some drugs.

[8]In their study of factors associated with material deprivation, Mayer and Jencks found that a family's access to credit was a stronger predictor of hardships than the family's income. Based on a regression study, they concluded:

> All else equal, a family's ability to borrow $500 had as much effect on hardship as multiplying its current income by a factor of three. . . . The extraordinary importance of access to credit is consistent with our unstructured interviews, in which many respondents imputed their hardships to unforeseen changes in income or expenses. [Mayer and Jencks 1989, p. 109]

While few people borrow $500 at pawnshops, access to emergency credit of smaller amounts may also avert serious hardship for many households.

assets of $150,000. In addition, in a county with a population of more than 250,000, the owner must show a public need for and probable profitability of an additional pawnshop. Such barriers to entry are in the interests of pawnbrokers—but not in the public interest. Where they do exist, there is a strong case for setting binding ceilings on pawnshop fees to prevent brokers from exploiting local monopoly power.[9]

Whatever the regulations a state decides to adopt, it is not enough merely to draft the regulations and expect them to be followed. Resources must also be devoted to publicizing the regulations and enforcing them. Very few states currently make any effort in this respect. In fact, in many states it is hard to find anyone in state government who is even aware of what the regulations are or to whom a customer should complain if the customer feels cheated. Because few state regulators ever patronize pawnshops themselves, it is critical to enforcement efforts that they make it easy for pawnshop customers to complain when they feel mistreated and to find out the key regulations. I would even suggest that regulators occasionally patronize pawnshops as customers to better understand the institutions that they oversee and to verify regulatory compliance.

Clearly, regulations should be drafted to minimize enforcement costs, which need not be high. Since there are undoubtedly economies of scale in regulation, smaller states might join with some of their neighbors in financing regulatory activities. Taking this approach, all states should be able to meet the costs of regulating the industry through modest annual license fees on pawnshops.

As part of the regulatory process, pawnbrokers should be required to file annual reports on their operations, providing information on the number of items pawned, the amount lent on pledges, the percentage of forfeits, and so forth. The regulators should use this information to produce public annual reports on the industry. This serves several purposes. It helps regulators identify irregularities in pawnshop operations that could be a signal of illegal activities. In addition, since the only organized group

---

[9]States that set ceilings on interest rates should either permit brokers to charge a fixed transaction fee in addition to the interest rate or permit a higher interest rate to be charged on small loans. Without such policies, brokers would refuse to make very small loans since there are fixed transaction costs to any loan regardless of its size.

that will actively follow the actions of state regulators will be pawnbrokers, there is always the danger that state regulators will hear only the pawnbrokers' concerns and may ultimately promote regulations that serve only the interest of the industry. Annual public reports can reduce the odds that this will occur, for anyone who is interested can monitor pawnshop activities. Annual reports could also serve as a source of information about social conditions in the state. Moreover, most pawnbrokers can provide this information at low cost since almost all have computerized their loan operations.

It is unlikely that any municipal or state government in America will want to follow the approach of many such governments in Continental Europe and Latin America and start their own not-for-profit pawnshops. In large cities, however, church groups or community development organizations that want to reduce the cost of pawnshop loans might try replicating the success of New York City's Provident Loan Society. As explained in Chapter 2, this not-for-profit organization operates several pawnshops making loans at an interest rate of 26 percent a year. It has a reputation for being scrupulously honest in its dealings with its customers. It is able to keep its fees so low because it is tax-exempt, it lends almost exclusively on watches and jewelry, and it makes only a small percentage of loans below $50. Such an approach may be feasible only in a densely populated urban area. It is, nevertheless, an idea that should be explored outside of New York. Such pawnshops should not, of course, be started without a careful feasibility study.[10]

THE REGULATION OF CHECK-CASHING OUTLETS

Check-cashing transactions are simpler than pawnshop loan transactions. A check-cashing transaction is completed with one

[10]It is interesting to note that the retired New York City pawnbroker, William Simpson, considered such an approach the best way to serve consumer interests.

. . . [I]n the future the hocker's problems will probably be best solved through such organizations as the Provident Loan Society of New York . . . for they are the most hopeful modern development in a field where the public for generations has been mauled, rooked and unmercifully exploited. [Simpson et al. 1954, p. 296] interaction between the customer and the store, and customers do not leave their property in the care of the CCO. This means that the regulatory needs for CCOs are much less than those for pawnshops.[11] This does not imply, however, that they should be completely unregulated. It is reasonable that the federal government, for example, in its efforts to reduce money laundering and tax evasion, requires CCOs and other financial institutions to file reports on large cash transactions. Furthermore, to reduce the odds that some CCOs, which handle a high volume of cash transactions, become controlled by criminal interests, states should require CCOs to be licensed and should ensure that CCO owners do not have criminal ties.

Although there is almost universal agreement that CCOs should be regulated sufficiently to prevent their use for criminal purposes, there is much disagreement over whether ceilings should be set on CCOs' check-cashing fees. Those advocating such controls generally make two points: (1) many check-cashing customers are relatively unsophisticated consumers with little social or economic power, who are sometimes grossly overcharged by unscrupulous operators; and (2) since many low- and moderate-income individuals spend a large percentage of their limited disposable incomes for basic financial transactions, CCO fee ceilings might ameliorate this situation.

There is evidence that some check-cashing firms levy relatively high fees. For example, the survey by the Consumer Federation of America (1989) found that 11 percent of CCOs nationwide charge 3 percent or more for cashing government entitlement checks. In my own survey of 42 check-cashing outlets across several states, I found three charging 5–6 percent to cash government and payroll checks. In New Jersey, where check cashers are limited by law to charging 1.0 percent on in-state checks and 1.5 percent on out-of-state checks, the New Jersey Department of the Public Advocate (1988, p. 29) found one case where a Hispanic woman who could not speak English was charged $25 for cashing a $268 social security check. Another woman was charged $16

---

[11] This assumes that the CCO does not make payday loans or cash postdated checks. If it does, the CCO is in the small loan business where the case for fairly extensive regulations and monitoring is strong.

for cashing her $525 AFDC check. In addition, households that regularly cash their paychecks at CCOs charging typical check-cashing fees of 1.5 to 2.5 percent devote a much larger share of their disposable incomes to basic payments services than do the vast majority of people using banks.

There are drawbacks to addressing these concerns through binding ceilings on check-cashing fees. For example, if low check-cashing rates are mandated, CCOs will refuse to cash riskier checks, such as personal checks or paychecks from small businesses. In addition, as with pawnshops, setting binding ceilings on check-cashing fees can put many CCOs out of business. With a low ceiling on CCO fees, only high-volume outlets will be able to cover their fixed costs. Consequently, it may be impossible for CCOs outside of heavily traveled urban areas to operate profitably. In New York, for example, the ceiling rate from 1988 to late 1992 was 0.9 percent or $0.50, whichever was greater. Although there were over 400 check-cashing outlets in the state, almost all of them were located in the New York City area. Similarly, CCOs in Illinois, which permits check cashers to charge up to 1.2 percent of the face value of the check plus $0.90, are heavily concentrated in the Chicago area.

Low ceiling rates, therefore, benefit consumers lucky enough to have convenient access to surviving outlets and who seek to cash low-risk checks, but they can make CCOs inaccessible to others. In fact, once customers' average transportation costs are included into the cost of using CCOs, lowering ceiling rates for check cashing can raise the cost of the service to some consumers. In the extreme, a very low ceiling on fees can completely kill the industry. Prior to 1989, for example, Delaware limited check-cashing outlets to a fee of 0.5 percent of the face value of a check or $0.25, whichever was greater. In 1989, the state, noting that there were no CCOs in the state operating under the old law, raised the limit to 1.0 percent or $4.00, whichever is greater.

One way to mandate lower rates without decimating the industry or significantly reducing the number of outlets is to permit CCOs to handle other profitable business. For example, a state might give CCOs the exclusive right to distribute automobile license plates for a fee in exchange for requiring them to also cash checks at low rates. Illinois and New York have taken some steps in this direction. Many CCOs in Illinois have the right to handle automobile registration and title transfers. Residents of New York City and Chicago can also elect to receive their AFDC payments or food stamps through a local CCO. In New York the state pays the CCO to distribute AFDC benefits in cash. In Illinois the CCOs handle the distribution of AFDC checks for free, but if the recipients cash their checks at the distributing CCO they must pay the regulated state fee.

An alternative approach, which some states have adopted and which I find reasonable, does not seek to lower the median check-cashing fee but does attempt to prevent CCOs from charging fees well above the average. The fee ceilings in California, Georgia, Minnesota, and Rhode Island, for example, are high enough so that they are unlikely to be binding for most check cashers (see Table 3.4). At the same time, the ceilings, if rigorously enforced, would prevent unscrupulous check cashers from charging less sophisticated customers or customers with no practical alternatives very high fees. Moreover, because the fee ceilings in these states have not forced most CCOs to lower their fees, they have not driven CCOs out of business, raising customers' transportation costs. One minor drawback to such ceilings, however, is that they might prevent CCOs from cashing high-risk checks or checks from people without satisfactory identification.

If fee ceilings are to protect the most vulnerable CCO customers, they must be actively enforced. In New Jersey, where check cashers are limited by law to charging 1.0 percent on in-state checks and 1.5 percent on out-of-state checks, the New Jersey Department of the Public Advocate (1988, p. 29) surveyed 662 customers and found that 49 percent were charged more than the legal maximum. On average, check cashers overcharged by about 44 percent of the ceiling rate. Interestingly, in its response to the study by the Department of the Public Advocate, the New Jersey Department of Banking, which oversees check-cashing outlets, reported that it had received only one check-cashing complaint in two years (U.S. GAO 1988, p. 9). Evidently, the vast majority of people who were charged more than the legal maximum in New Jersey did not complain to the oversight agency, perhaps because they were unaware of the overcharge, or believed that a complaint would be ineffective or not worth the effort, or perhaps they did not know how to file an official complaint.[12]

The higher the ceilings on CCO fees, the less incentive there is for CCOs to violate them. Thus, the costs for enforcing fee ceilings that are generally nonbinding should not be high. As a first step, a state must make CCO customers aware of the ceilings and provide the customers with a low-cost way to file complaints when they think the ceilings are violated. One way to do this would be to require CCOs to post a toll-free consumer complaint telephone number. The state must also devote resources to investigating complaints. Not every complaint must be investigated, but any CCO that is the subject of numerous complaints should be subject to close scrutiny. To lower enforcement costs and protect customers, all CCOs should be required to issue receipts that show the face value of the check, the amount and percentage charged, and the amount paid to the customer.

It is quite likely, in fact, that ceilings on check-cashing fees would be unnecessary if CCOs were required to post their rates prominently in simple terms and to issue receipts consistent with the posted rates. Regulators could draw up guidelines for exactly how rates should be posted to prevent a CCO from posting a confusing array of rates. In a completely unregulated market, the major potential for abuse arises if CCOs can vary the amount that they charge customers or can confuse customers about the charges. Requiring them to post rates and issue receipts, as grocery stores are commonly required to do, should stimulate competition among CCOs and prevent the most vulnerable customers from being victimized. To enforce the regulations, regulators must occasionally make unannounced visits to CCOs to verify that the rates are correctly posted and that customers are provided receipts matching the posted rates. Violations should result in substantial fines or the revocation of a CCO's license.

---

[12]The New Jersey Department of Banking told the New Jersey Department of the Public Advocate (1988, p. 68) that it relied on the "honor system" to assure compliance with state limits on check-cashing fees.

7 / Policies To Make Deposit Accounts More Accessible

Recognizing that a significant and growing number of households depend on pawnshops and check-cashing outlets for basic financial services, the previous chapter proposed some regulatory measures to protect fringe banking customers from potential abuse. This chapter examines policy proposals aimed at improving the financial and physical accessibility of deposit accounts for lower-income households. Such policies could complement efforts to improve the regulation of fringe banks and to increase the financial savings of the poor.

Most such proposals impose costs on banks. Some bankers have complained that it is unfair to require banks to serve perceived public interests when other retail businesses are not asked to do so. Such unequal treatment is justified, however, because the government provides banks with privileges that other businesses do not receive. For example, the government restricts entry into banking by requiring that depository institutions secure government charters, it insures banks deposits, and it permits depository institutions to borrow from Federal Reserve and Federal Home Loan Banks under special arrangements.

Although the government has the right to require banks to serve public interests, there are practical limits on the costs that can be imposed on banks. Bank owners must receive a fair risk-adjusted rate of return on their capital, or they will move their capital elsewhere. Moreover, banks cannot always count on passing on to their customers the costs associated with fulfilling government regulations. U.S. banks compete with offshore banks for very large deposits, and they compete domestically with money market mutual funds, mortgage companies, finance companies, securities markets, and with each other. The government must therefore ensure that it does not impose such heavy costs on banks that they are significantly disadvantaged relative to foreign banks or nonbank competitors. The government must also ensure that any public service obligations it imposes on banks are shared equally across banks, so that some banks are not placed at a competitive disadvantage relative to other banks.

"LIFELINE" BANKING

In response to evidence that fees on deposit accounts with small balances increased over the 1980s, federal legislators have introduced proposals to set ceilings on these fees. These efforts, known as "basic" or "lifeline" banking proposals, aim to ensure that bank accounts are affordable for low- and moderate-income families. Although there are many variations in the details of the proposals, they would all require banks to offer, for modest monthly fees, deposit accounts with low minimum-balance requirements and some checkwriting privileges. Other proposals would require banks to cash government assistance checks for nondepositors at no charge, or for nominal fees.[1]

A federal lifeline banking law would undoubtedly benefit some low-income households. Those now maintaining deposit accounts

---

[1]A few states have enacted basic banking laws of some form (Rubin 1992, pp. 216–217). Connecticut requires banks to cash government checks for nondepositors. Massachusetts has a similar requirement and requires state-chartered banks to provide no-fee savings and checking accounts to customers over 65 and under 18. Illinois requires banks to offer accounts with 10 free checks a month and a minimum initial deposit of $100 for customers over 65. Minnesota and Pennsylvania require banks that wish to engage in interstate banking to offer accounts with specified low-cost features.

with small balances in banks with comparatively high fees would realize savings. If banks were required to cash nondepositors' government support checks without charge, this could benefit individuals now paying for these services. In addition, some low-income households, which currently do not maintain deposit accounts, might find it advantageous to open them if account fees were reduced.

The banking industry has generally opposed lifeline banking legislation.[2] Industry representatives argue that lowering fees on bank accounts with small balances is unlikely to increase dramatically the ownership of bank accounts by lower-income families. The research presented in Chapter 5 supports this conclusion (see Table 5.7). Many people do not use savings institutions because they do not have any financial savings at the end of the pay period or because they prefer to transact almost exclusively in cash. Such individuals are unlikely to open bank accounts simply because the price of deposit accounts falls by a few dollars a month. On the other hand, about 15 percent of families without bank accounts identify bank service charges and minimum balance requirements as primary barriers to opening accounts. It is unlikely that all of these families would open accounts if fees were lowered, but, even if only half did, that would make a substantial contribution to increasing account ownership.

Critics of lifeline banking proposals also charge that there is no evidence of market failure in the pricing of bank services. It is argued therefore that concerns about the economic accessibility of bank accounts for lower-income households ought to be addressed by income transfers to such households, not by legislation forcing banks to lower fees on deposit accounts. Addressing the problem by forcing banks to offer lifeline banking services is wasteful from two perspectives. First, artificially lowering the

---

[2] Among other things, representatives of the banking industry have argued that lifeline banking legislation is unnecessary because most banks already voluntarily offer lifeline accounts. But their data on the number of banks currently offering lifeline accounts are usually based on a rather unrestrictive definition of what constitutes a lifeline account. They also fail to distinguish between the percentage of banks in affluent areas offering such accounts and the percentage in low-income areas. It would do little good if all the banks in Scarsdale, New York, for example, offered lifeline accounts and none in the Bronx did.

price of some bank services encourages consumers to overuse these resources. For example, it cost about $0.40 (in 1991 prices) for the banking system to process a check in 1986 (Humphrey and Berger 1990). If banks are not permitted to charge for checks on lifeline accounts, consumers with such accounts might write checks for very small payments that could just as easily be paid with cash. Second, although lifeline banking proposals intend to transfer benefits to low-income consumers, most of the proposals call for fees to be lowered on particular types of accounts and do not specifically target low-income consumers. Benefits are bound to be transferred to some middle- and high-income families. Social security checks, for example, go to almost all people over 65, whether they are rich or poor. If a lifeline banking law requires banks to cash nondepositors' government checks without charge, all social security recipients would be eligible to receive an implicit subsidy in cashing their checks. Similarly, anyone could open a subsidized lifeline account, even children from affluent families or a wealthy person whose liquid assets are kept in a money market mutual fund.

These criticisms are not sufficient to reject all lifeline banking proposals. Although it might be better to address the economic difficulties of low-income families through income transfers and job creation, this is unlikely to receive broad political support. Because lifeline banking subsidizes the use of an approved service and because its financial costs to the general public are hidden, it is more likely to be politically popular. In addition, although lifeline accounts will undoubtedly benefit some middle- and upper-income people, this could be limited by designing the accounts so that they are desirable only to those with quite modest financial savings and limited needs for payment transactions.[3] For example, lifeline accounts might pay no interest on deposit balances and permit the account holder to write only a small number of free

---

[3]Legislation could require households to meet income criteria to be eligible for a lifeline account, but the administrative costs of such an approach are likely to be unreasonable. Limiting lifeline accounts to those over age 65 is a low-cost alternative, and some states have taken this approach. However, a much higher percentage of people over 65 have bank accounts than do younger people (see Table 5.1).

checks a month. Account holders might also be restricted to a limited number of free teller interactions per month.

The most serious criticism of a lifeline banking law is that it would place an uneven economic burden on banks. Banks with a large share of their branches in low-income areas would face much higher costs from implementing the law than would banks with all of their branches in affluent areas. Moreover, a bank with large numbers of lifeline accounts or numerous nondepositors seeking to cash government checks may not be able to pass on the costs of these services to its other customers by lowering interest rates on large deposit accounts or raising rates on loans. If it tried to do so, many of its customers might move to other banks or to nonbank competitors, such as money market mutual funds, mortgage institutions, or business and personal finance companies. Banks with a large share of their branches in low-income areas might be forced to close some or all of these branches to survive.

This problem could be avoided if proper care is taken in drafting lifeline banking regulations. Regulations on lifeline accounts should seek to keep the costs to consumers of such accounts low, but not so low as to impose a heavy financial burden on banks. Rather than requiring banks to cash government entitlement checks for free, for example, lifeline regulations might require banks to cash the checks but permit them to charge a small fee for the service. To reduce the financial burden on banks cashing large numbers of government checks or handling numerous lifeline accounts, the government could offer financial incentives to banks that devote more than a given percentage of their business to these activities. Such a program could be financed through a small tax on all deposit institutions as well as, perhaps, on nonbank competitors, including money market mutual funds and mortgage and finance companies.

Balancing these considerations, I conclude that a moderate lifeline banking law would be good public policy. Such a law would ensure that low-income households with modest financial savings can afford to safeguard their funds in a deposit account with a reasonable range of associated payment services. The cost of the required account subsidies would be quite modest under the more moderate lifeline banking proposals. Moreover, legislation might be drafted so that these costs would be spread across all financial institutions.

THE COMMUNITY REINVESTMENT ACT
AND BANK REPRESENTATION
IN LOW-INCOME AND MINORITY COMMUNITIES

Requiring banks to offer lifeline accounts is, at the time of this writing, merely a legislative proposal. The major existing legislation governing banks' services to low-income and minority communities is the Community Reinvestment Act (CRA), which aims to ensure that banks do not engage in "redlining," meaning that a bank routinely provides less credit to individuals from poor or minority neighborhoods than to individuals with similar risk characteristics from other communities. Although data limitations prevent researchers from proving conclusively that banks have discriminated across communities in providing housing or business loans, mortgage data from a variety of urban areas have been consistent with that conclusion (Campen 1993).

Redlining patterns might reflect racial discrimination or might result from profit-maximizing behavior if banks find it more costly to assess the credit risk of borrowers from low-income or minority communities. Redlining could also emerge if the success of a bank's loans within a community depends on how many other banks are lending to that community. In this case, a profit-maximizing bank would lend to communities in which other banks are also lending. If all banks behave this way, some communities may be starved for credit, resulting in a decline in their property values and business activities.

Wherever redlining does exist, whatever its cause, it is clearly appropriate that the government intervene. The CRA does provide bank regulators with the powers for this purpose. The CRA was initially enacted in 1977, but its requirements were vague and it was given little attention by regulators or bankers. In 1989, the Act was revised to set more specific requirements for banks and to ensure that regulators monitored and encouraged banks' compliance. The revised CRA became effective in mid-1990.

Under current CRA legislation, a bank must supply regulators with a variety of information documenting the extent to which it is striving to meet the legitimate credit needs of all members of the communities it serves. Based on this information, the regulators annually review a bank's performance against twelve criteria and issue a CRA rating of "outstanding," "satisfactory," "needs to improve," or "substantial noncompliance." There are no direct sanctions associated with receiving a poor CRA rating, but a bank's CRA record is considered when regulators decide whether to permit the bank to establish a new branch, move an existing office, or to merge with or acquire another financial institution.[4] In addition, the CRA evaluations are publicized, a measure intended to increase the pressure on banks to seek favorable ratings. Since the tougher CRA guidelines became effective only in mid-1990, it is too early to know whether they will significantly affect bank activities in minority and low-income urban areas.

The CRA also has a provision intended to pressure banks to maintain branch offices in these communities.[5] One of the twelve bank-evaluating criteria is: "The institution's record of opening and closing offices and providing services at offices" (Federal Financial Institutions Examination Council 1992, p. 6). In applying the provision, regulators have required banks to define a geographic area of operation around their current branches. The location of existing branches and their geographic areas of operation should not be gerrymandered to exclude low-income areas. If it appears that they are, the bank might need to open branches in low-income or minority areas to ensure that it receives a satisfactory CRA rating. In addition, regulators have interpreted the provision to mean that closings of bank branches should not impact disproportionately on low-income or minority areas.

---

[4]This was also true under the 1977 version of the CRA, but CRA evaluations received little weight in regulators' decisions. Since the mid-1990s, CRA evaluations have received more weight and banks have worked to ensure that they receive at least a "satisfactory" rating. After the standards were toughened in 1989, banks' applications for mergers or other changes were denied on a few occasions due to unsatisfactory CRA records (Skidmore 1989; Bacon and Wilke 1993).

[5]Some states have also passed laws intended to slow any exodus of banks from low-income areas. New York law, for example, requires banks and thrifts to notify their customers and appropriate regulators 180 days prior to a bank closing in order to give community groups and regulators time to analyze the closing and, if appropriate, oppose it.

There are two justifications for this provision. First, if banks have physical "bricks and mortar" representation in a community, this is likely to enhance credit flows for local small businesses and housing needs. The second justification is based on payments and savings services: households and businesses will find it more convenient and less costly to maintain deposit accounts and use related payment services if a bank branch is nearby.

Representatives of the banking industry have complained about many aspects of the CRA, but they have been especially critical of the provision pressuring banks to open or maintain branches in low-income or minority communities. For example, industry representatives have complained that the CRA, as currently written, is unfair to some banks and could be counterproductive. Bankers have argued that, to the extent that the CRA limits bank branch closings in low-income and minority communities, it can place an unfair burden on banks with existing offices in such areas. Presumably, suburban banks that never entered these communities will remain free to open and close offices at will. Over the long run, the CRA might also be counterproductive: If bankers believe that offices they open in low-income communities cannot be closed in the future without endangering their CRA ratings, they may be unwilling to open the offices in the first place.

These criticisms do call for modification of the CRA. For example, the government could require banks, *wherever they are located*, to demonstrate a commitment to assist in economic development efforts in low-income communities. Under a modified CRA, banks without branches near low-income communities might join a consortia of banks that jointly capitalize and operate a branch in an underserved area. To lower costs and provide more effective credit services, the consortia should probably include a bank with operating experience in the designated low-income area or in related areas. To prevent the CRA from having a counterproductive effect, it is important that regulators permit banks that voluntarily open branches in low-income areas to close those branches if they are insufficiently profitable. In other words, regulators should demand from all banks a continuing commitment to assist economic development efforts in low-income areas, but not signal to banks that particular efforts are irreversible or immutable.

In future efforts to assure that savings and payment services are available in all communities, the government ought to consider separating policies to address this issue from policies promoting business and housing credit in low-income and minority communities. The former goal is more limited and, therefore, less costly. It could be appropriate in some communities that cannot support a full-service bank branch. The federal government, for example, might encourage the establishment of community credit unions in neighborhoods lacking deposit services. In some cases, a credit union can flourish where banks cannot because credit unions face lower regulatory requirements and receive tax advantages. A credit union cannot meet all of the credit needs related to economic development, but it could provide consumer loans and meet the need for the safekeeping of financial savings and associated payment services. Banks might play a role in this process if they could partially fulfill their CRA obligations by providing technical or financial assistance to credit unions serving low-income or minority communities.

A more radical idea, one that merits serious consideration in policy-making circles, would be to allow check-cashing outlets to function as agents for banks and take deposits. A CCO could offer regular fee-based payment services to customers without deposit accounts while providing a bank's payment services to those with accounts. This would permit people who live in communities without bank branches to obtain bank payment and deposit services locally while saving banks the cost of establishing a full-service branch. Such an approach should not, of course, excuse banks from the obligation to ensure that credit is available in low-income and minority communities for legitimate business and housing needs.

There are some precedents for this idea.[6] France's largest bank, *Credit Agricole,* recently signed up 10,000 bakers, butchers, and grocers in rural areas to serve as limited agents for the bank (*The Economist* 9/21/91). They cash checks, take deposits, and arrange money transfers, getting paid 3 francs for each transaction. In a recent article, Edward Rubin (1992) proposed that supermarket chains be permitted to serve as bank branch locations or begin operating as depository institutions themselves. CCOs are proba-

---

[6]This idea was first suggested to me by Hyman Minsky.

bly a better choice, however, because they are designed to handle large amounts of cash securely and are more likely to be located in economically depressed neighborhoods.

Such a proposal would require a number of critical details to be worked out. A policy to permit CCOs to accept deposits might apply across a state or nationwide, or it might be permitted only in designated geographic areas. For simplicity, CCOs might be permitted to accept only passbook savings deposits. A CCO's correspondent bank could place an ATM in the CCO, paying the CCO a fee for the space. On specified days of the week, the bank could send a representative to the CCO to take loan applications and answer questions. If CCOs were to function as deposit intermediaries for banks, they would have to be compensated for this function. This could be covered by fees on customers' accounts or on their transactions. For low-income customers, some of these fees, or perhaps even all, might be covered by the bank. Banks' interest in such linkages would be enhanced if they found this a low-cost means of partially satisfying the requirements of the Community Reinvestment Act.

A POSTAL SAVINGS SYSTEM

As an alternative to using regulations and subsidies to address problems with bank branch locations and fees on small accounts, the federal government could itself provide basic financial services. Since post offices already exist in most communities, they are a natural location to offer such services. Moreover, using post offices would avoid the cost of having to create government financial centers *de novo*. Although this idea may initially appear radical, it seems less so when it is recognized that most other industrialized countries take this approach and that the United States has in the past.

Japan and most West European countries operate postal savings systems. People can open savings accounts at post offices and make third party payments by postal money order or by electronically transferring funds from their accounts to the postal accounts of others, including the power company, the telephone company, etc. To keep postal savings operations simple, check-writing privileges are generally not offered, nor does the postal savings system make loans. The postal systems commonly permit customers to open only savings accounts; the deposited funds are invested in government treasury bills and bonds. In Japan and Europe, it is generally moderate-income people and people in isolated rural areas who keep accounts at the post office. The more affluent and urban dwellers prefer the wider range of services offered at commercial or savings banks.

The United States had a postal savings system from 1910 to 1966 (O'Hara and Easley 1979) specifically designed to provide banking facilities in areas without banks and to appeal to small savers, especially immigrants who distrusted banks and were accustomed to European postal savings systems. It was abolished in 1966 because after World War II its deposit base fell to very low levels. This decline was probably due to two factors: first, private banks gained federal deposit insurance in the early 1930s, which meant that an account in a private bank was as secure as an account at the post office; second, postal savings accounts paid only a 2 percent annual interest rate, which compared unfavorably with the rates paid on savings accounts at banks and savings and loans after World War II.

If the United States were to revive its postal savings system, this could be done either nationally or at selected post offices. As in Europe, the postal savings system would presumably permit people to open savings accounts, purchase money orders, and make some electronic payments. People with or without accounts could cash government support checks. The post office could also join a regional ATM network to offer depositors 24-hour access to their funds.

A proposal to revive the U.S. postal savings system is worthy of study. I suspect, however, that reopening the postal savings system would not be the most cost-effective way to address problems with the accessibility of bank accounts for low-income families. Preparing post offices to handle the new business could require significant investments in physical and human capital. The same goal can almost certainly be accomplished at a lower cost by providing incentives for financial institutions, which already have the physical and human capital in place, to address it.

Concluding
Comments

Over the 1980s, the number of pawnshops and check-cashing outlets nationwide more than doubled. In the first section of this
chapter, I argue that this growth is likely to continue into the
1990s, albeit at a slower pace. I also consider the possibility that
banks might enter the fringe banking market. In the second section, I discuss some economic and social implications of the growing segmentation of consumer financial markets. In the context of
this discussion, I return to the four themes set out in the first
chapter.

THE FUTURE OF FRINGE BANKING

Pawnbroking may have reached a saturation point in several
southern states, but it clearly has tremendous potential growth in
the Northeast and Great Lakes states. To open up these markets,
however, will require regulatory changes in states with relatively
tight usury ceilings. This observation has not been lost on the
industry. As one would expect, pawnbrokers are actively pushing
for more favorable regulations. In many states they have formed
professional associations and hired lobbyists. In fact, the growth

of the industry has reinforced attempts to make pawnshop laws more favorable to the industry, since the chains and large active state associations have far more political clout than did the unorganized mom-and-pop stores that used to dominate fringe banking. And the industry's efforts to change state laws are producing results: between 1989 and mid-1993 at least four states revised their pawnshop laws to make them more favorable to the industry.

In the short term, there are probably also good growth prospects for check-cashing outlets. CCOs are well represented in Chicago and New York City but still comparatively rare in many promising markets of numerous cities. In all but three or four states, regulations are not as great a barrier to further expansion as is the need to familiarize potential customers with CCO services in areas where they are not well established. Inadequate bank financing can be an additional barrier, especially where banks are unfamiliar with CCO operations. However, the rise of large, well-capitalized and professionally managed chains is overcoming these impediments to the expansion of the industry.

Although the short-term outlook for CCOs is favorable, the long-run perspective may not be. The main threat comes from changes in payment practices. In an attempt to reduce processing costs and the risks associated with delivering and receiving government assistance payments, governments at all levels have been experimenting with electronic delivery of benefits. In a few cases, governments have issued recipients encoded debit cards which closely resemble credit cards. They are linked to an account that is credited each month with the appropriate government assistance payment, and cardholders can use them to spend up to this monthly limit. The cards can be used in point-of-sale terminals to pay for goods at selected local merchants or, in some cases, to withdraw cash from ATM networks. A second development that threatens CCOs is the growing use of electronic means to deliver salaries. A trade organization, the National Automated Clearing House Association, reports that in 1992 about 30 percent of salaries were paid by direct deposit into employees' bank accounts. A decade earlier, less than 5 percent were.

Over the long run these developments are likely to slow or even reverse the growth of the check-cashing industry, but their short-run impact can easily be exaggerated. Many CCOs mainly cash paychecks and do not depend heavily on the fees generated from cashing government benefit checks. In fact, about 75–90 percent of the checks that New York CCOs cashed in 1989 were payroll checks (Reeb et al. 1991, p. C-15). In addition, in some areas of the country that have introduced electronic delivery of government assistance, CCOs participate in the program. The CCOs receive a small fee for serving as delivery points for the wired funds. Although electronic paycheck deposits are growing rapidly, they are unlikely to include in the near future a significant share of households without bank accounts. State laws commonly do not permit employers to mandate that their employees use direct deposit. And many employers have resisted switching to direct deposit because they gain interest (float) on payroll funds until paychecks clear through the banking system. Many employers, especially those with hourly or low-wage employees, also report that they fear that a significant share of their employees would protest a change to direct deposit.

In considering the future of fringe banking, another looming question is whether the national and regional chains will come to dominate the field. Although well-managed independent stores will certainly survive for the foreseeable future, I expect that the chains will increasingly dominate both pawnbroking and commercial check cashing. Several considerations lead to this conclusion. First, in pawnbroking there are some economies of scale and gains from brand name identification. Unredeemed collateral can be easily reallocated among shops to promote sales. Customers must trust a broker to take good care of their collateral, so it is reasonable to expect that, when moving to new areas, customers will tend to choose a shop that is part of a chain with a national or regional reputation for responsible business behavior. Second, since access to outside financing is often critical to the success of both pawnshops and CCOs, professionally managed chains with comprehensive accounting records are more likely to obtain access to bank credit and other sources of financing than are the typical owner-operated stores.

Looking ahead, one can easily imagine mainstream banks entering the fringe banking field. Prospects for this development seem greatest in the case of commercial check cashing. Check cashers must clear checks through the banking system, and they require periodic access to substantial volumes of cash. Banks have the cash as well as direct access to check-clearing procedures. Moreover, in recent years banks have moved toward charging explicit fees for the services they provide. Completing this process, by providing payment services unbundled from deposit services, would not be a big step. In fact, at the time of this writing, at least two banks, one based in Chicago and the other in San Francisco, have recently begun to offer fee-based check-cashing services for nondepositors.

There are, on the other hand, reasons to doubt that more than a handful of intrepid banks would enter commercial check cashing. Bank tellers have not been trained to determine at a glance a check's payment risk since this is largely irrelevant under existing bank policies. Although banks could remedy this problem, they would probably hesitate to provide a fee-based check-cashing service in the same lobby serving depositors, for they might fear that their customers with deposit accounts would prefer, for reasons of status or other motives, to be served separately from customers seeking only payment services. Banks might also worry that if they begin to charge explicit fees for cashing checks for nondepositors, this could prompt charges that they are exploiting the poor, thereby increasing political pressure to regulate all bank fees more stringently. In fact, when a San Francisco-based bank began to offer commercial check-cashing services in the Los Angeles area, it was criticized as "ripping off" the poor (Richtel 1993).

These considerations suggest that, if large numbers of banks do enter commercial check cashing, they will do so through subsidiaries with corporate names that differ from the banks' names. These subsidiaries would operate CCOs located separately from a parent bank's branches. Such an approach would allow banks to operate CCOs without endangering carefully nurtured corporate images.

Banks are much less likely to enter the pawnbroking market directly. Although banks have ready access to substantial funds for loans, the skills required to run a successful pawnshop differ substantially from banking skills. Few bank loan officers, for example, could quickly place a value on a used rifle, television set, or diamond ring. Moreover, pawnshops have a longstanding unsavory popular reputation, which might make banks hesitate to associate closely with them. As pawnshop chains continue to grow, however, large financial institutions might conceivably invest in them. This would enable these institutions to share in the profits without being open to the charge that they directly make loans to low-income individuals at annual interest rates of over 200 percent. In fact, a large Los Angeles bank and a British insurance company already own a significant share of Cash America Investments, the largest national pawnshop chain.

A RETURN TO THE FOUR THEMES

The share of the population operating outside of the main stream financial system grew markedly over the 1980s. As a result, the contemporary consumer financial system is noticeably more segmented. The vast majority of households obtain credit and payment services through banks, savings and loans, or credit unions. A large minority, however, obtain basic financial services from pawnshops and check-cashing outlets.

As noted in the first theme of Chapter 1, most of the households using fringe banks have low or moderate incomes, and they pay far more for basic financial services than do the generally more affluent households using deposit institutions. Although family income is correlated with the use of fringe banks, a stronger determinant is a family's ability to maintain financial savings, which is related to family income, income stability, family structure, special needs, and lifestyle choices. Since households that are unable to maintain financial savings are often excluded from the payment and credit services of deposit institutions, they turn to fringe banks to meet these needs. This is an expensive alternative, however, largely because pawnshops' and CCOs' operating costs are high relative to the size and volume of their transactions.

Some readers might argue that the consumer financial system has always been segmented and that the poor have always paid more for financial services, especially credit. This, however, misses two important points. First, from a long-term perspective the cost of operating outside of the banking system has increased. Consider, for example, payments. In the early part of this century, employers could not assume that the majority of their workers had bank accounts. Accordingly, they commonly paid their workers in cash. The workers in turn generally paid all of their bills, including their rents, in cash. The payments system thus imposed few costs on households operating on a cash basis.

The credit system did impose costs, but they were small compared to those of today. At the turn of the century, pawnshops flourished, providing loans on a wide range of collateral at annualized interest rates of between 30–50 percent. Although these interest rates were 25–45 percentage points higher than those of banks, pawnshop interest rates now are often 140–230 percentage points higher than rates on consumer loans at banks.

The main reason that the payments system has become more costly for individuals who operate on a cash-only basis is that such individuals have become a minority over the past century, and society no longer adjusts to accommodate them. In 1900, workers were paid in cash because employers knew that few of them had bank accounts. By 1980, employers assumed that most or all of their workers had accounts and preferred paychecks to cash.

Pawnshops, on the other hand, became significantly more expensive than banks largely due to changes in technology and productivity. At the turn of the century, banks maintained records by hand, and each credit decision was based on the data collected by a loan officer. Since the advent of the computer, banks have progressively substituted automation for human labor. Today, banks provide most small personal loans through credit cards, and computers do the credit screening and handle billing. Pawnshops have not been able to make a similar substitution of technology for human labor. In addition, the general increase in productivity of the labor force over the twentieth century has increased real wages, raising the relative cost of labor-intensive services.

The observation that the consumer financial system has always been segmented misses a second point as well: The increase over the 1980s in the percentage of the population operating on a cash-only basis reversed an earlier trend toward decreasing segmentation of financial markets. For example, the Federal Reserve Board's 1950 Survey of Consumer Finances found that 31 percent of American households had no financial assets other than cash

(Board of Governors 1960). By the 1977 survey, only 10 percent of households fell into this category (Board of Governors 1977). In the 1989 survey, however, 12.5 percent of households reported that they had no financial assets (Kennickell and Shack-Marquez 1992).

The second theme in Chapter 1 is that the increasing segmentation of the financial system largely reflects an increasing segmentation in the economic well-being of American families. The 1980s boom in fringe banking was mainly caused by an increase in the number of households living from paycheck to paycheck with no financial savings of note. Bank payment services are commonly restricted to bank depositors, so people without financial savings had to turn elsewhere for basic payment services. They were often forced to look elsewhere to meet their credit needs. Credit from mainstream financial institutions is offered only to individuals who can pass a credit-risk assessment; and households with low incomes and without bank accounts are significantly less likely to pass such a screening than others. In addition, any small past interruption in the incomes of these families or unexpected expenditures would have likely impeded their ability to pay their rents or to service existing debts, resulting in impaired credit records.

Changes in banking regulations and bank policies also contributed to the segmentation of consumer financial markets. The more widespread use of minimum-balance requirements and increased fees on small accounts undoubtedly prompted some individuals with modest savings to leave the banking system. This was probably not a major factor behind the growth of CCOs because, even with increases in bank fees, CCOs are a more expensive option than banks. Rather, most of those who closed accounts due to fee increases were probably able to cash their checks for free or at low cost elsewhere, perhaps at a retail store. On the other hand, the fee increases certainly could have spurred the demand for pawnshop services, since individuals without deposit accounts would be less likely to pass a credit-risk screening at mainstream financial institutions.

In some urban areas, banks closed branches disproportionately in low-income and African American communities over the 1980s, leaving many without any deposit institutions. In these communities, this would have contributed to a decline in the ownership of bank accounts and increased the demand for fringe banking services. Nationwide, however, bank branch closings were probably not a major factor behind the growth of fringe banking.

When I have presented these ideas in conversations, the reactions that I get seem to depend on the background of the listeners. People who live outside of the major urban areas in the Northeast and Midwest rarely challenge me, for they are used to seeing check-cashing outlets and pawnshops located in close proximity to banks. Moreover, they frequently drive by fringe banks along heavily traveled roads and see customers' cars and pick-up trucks parked out front. Given this experience, they quickly accept my conclusion that it is not a change in the physical accessibility of bank branches that is the driving force behind fringe banking.

I am, on the other hand, commonly challenged by people from the older major cities of the Northeast and Midwest. They argue that there are large sections of their cities, primarily those with significant concentrations of African Americans, in which bank branches are very rare and check-cashing outlets and pawnshops are common. I live in one of these northeastern cities and I do not disagree. I do point out, however, that even in these cities there are numerous fringe banks that thrive in close proximity to banks.

Although many people use fringe banks because they have no realistic alternative, the third theme of Chapter 1 emphasized that a significant share of pawnshop and CCO customers use them on a discretionary basis. For reasons given in Chapter 4, uncovering the exact percentages of necessitous and discretionary customers is not possible. However, available evidence strongly indicates that discretionary customers are not unusual, even among low- and moderate-income clients.

Among households using CCOs for check cashing because they cannot maintain sufficient savings to justify a deposit account are found low-wage workers who are barely able to support their families as well as young single workers who spend all of their discretionary income on clothes, jewelry, or sports cars. In addition, some CCO customers say that they use check-cashing outlets simply because they are convenient or because they like to get cash for their checks right away. In the case of pawnshops, although a high percentage of loan clients report that they patronize pawnshops for lack of alternatives, some also freely acknowledge that they are borrowing to pay for an unnecessary expenditure, such as a night out on the town. Other customers report that their loans are for necessary expenditures, but that past discretionary budgeting choices created their present cash shortfalls.

I tread carefully in making these points because they are sensitive. Political conservatives have sometimes used such observations to claim that many low-income people could climb out of poverty, if only they did not exhibit such shortsighted behavior. Some liberals, on the other hand, deny that the behavior of low-income households contributes in any way to their hardship. To avoid providing supporting evidence for such conservatives or offending some liberals, it might be best to ignore the discretionary use of fringe banks by lower-income households altogether. This would be a mistake, however, for it would leave a misleading impression of the diversity of fringe banking customers. Fortunately sociologists and urban anthropologists have begun to discuss shortsighted or even self-destructive behavior on the part of some lower-income individuals, while making it clear that they are not arguing that such behavior is the cause of poverty. Rather, they argue that the economic insecurity, limited educational opportunities, and powerlessness that often accompany poverty shape behavior.

Some readers might also object to my argument that fringe banking fees must be higher than the fees for similar services from mainstream financial institutions. This does not imply that we should be unconcerned about the segmentation of financial markets and the high fees for fringe banking services. If the poor must pay more for basic financial services, this increases the material hardship associated with poverty and makes it more difficult for the poor to raise their economic status. Additionally, the higher fees paid by the poor creates a perception that the financial system discriminates invidiously, and that the poor are preyed upon by more powerful economic interests. In the United States, where certain racial and ethnic groups are disproportionately represented among the poor, this can be particularly divisive.

These concerns justify governmental and private-sector efforts to address the problem. Since it costs less to deliver payment services to families with financial savings and credit services to families with steady incomes and good credit records, the most effective public policies to reduce the cost of financial services for low- and moderate-income families would be those that increase the ability of these families to save and stabilize their earnings. Expanding the earned income tax credit, a federal subsidy for low-wage workers, would certainly increase the standard of living of many low-income households and help them to accumulate modest savings. Maintaining high levels of aggregate employment, along with public work programs targeted at population groups suffering well-above-average levels of unemployment, would further help to increase and stabilize the earnings of lower-income households. Although such steps would probably do the most to benefit low-wage workers and reduce their spending on basic financial services, they may be politically unrealistic in the short term. This does not mean, however, that nothing useful can be done until the political basis for such programs develops. In particular, I advocate that we make efforts in three areas.

First, we ought to continue to strive to ensure that deposit institutions are accessible and affordable to families with limited savings. A moderate lifeline banking law could help in this regard and would not impose excessive costs on banks. In addition, we should continue to require banks to contribute to efforts to maintain bank branches in low-income and minority communities. Serious consideration should also be given to spreading the cost of these efforts to nonbank financial institutions. In those low-income communities where the demand for banks' savings and credit services is insufficient to justify a full-service bank branch, community credit unions may be able to meet many of the needs for financial services at a lower cost. In such communities, we might also consider permitting check-cashing outlets to affiliate with banks and take deposits.

A second policy initiative ought to focus on expanding consumer education opportunities for lower-income families. An effective program should be tailored specifically to the lives of the people enrolled, perhaps based on courses offered through schools, community development groups, church groups, or local civic organizations. An appropriate course might contrast the cost of fringe banking services with the cost of similar services at mainstream financial institutions. The course could also help consumers to clear up outstanding credit problems, teach money management skills, discuss the economics of rent-to-own contracts, and investigate price/quality trade-offs at local merchants.

Consumer education efforts are relatively low cost, but they are also likely to have only a modest impact on the lives of lower-income individuals. Realistically, the major problem that the vast majority of such individuals face is that of low and unstable incomes. Nevertheless, consumer education might help many lower-income households to improve family budgeting choices and to maintain low-cost deposit accounts, thereby freeing resources for higher priority uses. The experience of some not-for-profit community development agencies working to provide low-income housing corroborates my strong impression that there is a useful role for consumer education. In recent years, many such groups have settled on a two-pronged strategy (Wayne 1992). First, they work with governments, foundations, banks, and builders to create housing accessible to moderate- and low-income families. Second, they counsel potential homeowners to help them clear up past debt problems and to devise and maintain budgets to pay for their houses and future maintenance expenses. The groups have found that the ability of the families to purchase and maintain their homes is greatly enhanced by the financial counseling.

A third policy initiative should be to improve the regulation and monitoring of the fringe banking industry. Pawnshops and check-cashing outlets play an important role in the financial system. In fact, they may well be the most important financial institutions in the daily lives of millions of low- and moderate-income individuals. Although most states have extensive regulations for pawnshops, very few devote any resources to publicizing or enforcing the regulations. A minority of states regulate check-cashing outlets, and even fewer of those that do monitor regulatory compliance. Such patterns stand in stark contrast to the substantial resources devoted to regulating and monitoring the financial institutions in which the more affluent and more politically powerful interact.

The effective regulation of pawnshops and CCOs need not be costly, either to fringe banks or to taxpayers. The most important regulations are those that limit fringe banks to a simple set of financial services with terms that are easily understood, prominently posted, and universally applied. And some resources must be devoted to enforcing the regulations. Where check cashing is competitive and where such regulations are enforced, ceilings on fees are of secondary importance, and probably unnecessary. In the case of pawnshops, where some customers may be highly necessitous, moderate fee ceilings are probably an appropriate means of restraining unscrupulous brokers. In either case, wherever there are significant barriers to entry into fringe banking, fee ceilings are also justified. However, very low ceilings can drive pawnshops and CCOs out of business, leaving their customers with less desirable alternatives for credit and payment services.

Our society has devoted few resources to regulating and monitoring fringe banks because their customers have little weight in the economic and political system. This observation makes the protection of pawnshop and CCO customers all the more important. It could also create the impression that the prospects for reform are dim. I do not agree. The boom in fringe banking is forcing policymakers to recognize a traditionally neglected segment of the financial system. Activists in low-income communities and academics studying poverty are also becoming increasingly aware of how the poor interact with the financial system, and many are pushing for regulatory reforms.

Fringe bankers have created effective lobbies in many states, but pawnbrokers and commercial check cashers are themselves divided over regulatory issues. Predictably, many oppose any regulatory changes aside from those that simply relax existing restrictions. A significant number, however, believe that fringe banking's long-run prospects will be brighter if it is perceived as forthright and trustworthy in its dealings with customers. Forces outside of the industry, seeking to improve the regulation of fringe banks, may be able to work with these pawnbrokers and check cashers to obtain effective reforms.

Despite their use by millions of Americans, pawnshops and check-cashing outlets are a largely hidden part of our financial system. If this book accomplishes nothing else, it should at least bring these fringe banks into full view and lead to an overdue recognition of their role in that system.

Bibliography

Andreasen, Alan R. *The Disadvantaged Consumer.* (New York: Free Press, 1975).

Avery, Robert B. "Deregulation and the Location of Financial Institution Offices." Federal Reserve Bank of Cleveland *Economic Review* 27 (3) (1991): 30–42.

———, et al. "The Use of Cash and Transaction Accounts by American Families." *Federal Reserve Bulletin* (February 1986): 87–108.

Bacon, Kenneth H., and John R. Wilke. "Fed Gives Bias Laws New Clout as It Blocks a Bank Acquisition." *Wall Street Journal*, November 17, 1993.

Banfield, Edward. *The Unheavenly City Revisited.* (Boston: Little, Brown & Company, 1974).

Bartlett, Sarah. "Bank Closings Discriminate, Report Asserts." *New York Times.* January 30, 1989.

Bauman, F. J. A., and R. Houtman. "Pawnbroking as an Instrument of Rural Banking in the Third World." *Economic Development and Cultural Change* 37 (October 1988): 69–89.

Board of Governors of the Federal Reserve System. *Survey of Consumer Finances.* (Washington DC: Federal Reserve, 1960).

———. *1977 Consumer Credit Survey.* (Washington DC: Federal Reserve, 1977).

———. "Annual Report to the Congress on Retail Fees and Services of Depository Institutions." June 1992.

Brown, James L. "Problems in Defining and Representing 'The Consumer Interest.'" *Journal of Retail Banking* 8 (3) (Fall 1986): 53–58.

Campen, James T. "Banks, Communities, and Public Policy." In Dymski, Gary, et al. (eds.) *Restructuring the U.S. Monetary and Financial System.* (New York: M.E. Sharpe, 1993).

Canner, Glenn, and Ellen Maland. "Basic Banking." *Federal Reserve Bulletin* (April 1987): 255–269.

Caplovitz, David. *The Poor Pay More; Consumer Practices of Low-Income Families.* (New York: Free Press of Glencoe, 1963).

Caskey, John. "Pawnbroking in America: The Economics of a Forgotten Credit Market." *Journal of Money, Credit, and Banking* 23 (1) (February 1991): 85–99.

———. "Check-Cashing Outlets in the U.S. Financial System." Federal Reserve Bank of Kansas City *Economic Review* (November/December 1991): 53–67.

———. "Bank Representation in Low-Income and Minority Urban Communities." *Urban Affairs Quarterly* 29 (4) (June 1994): 617–638.

Caskey, John, and Andrew Peterson. "Who Has a Bank Account and Who Doesn't." *Eastern Economic Journal* 20 (1) (Winter 1994): 61–74.

Caskey, John, and Brian Zikmund. "Pawnshops: The Consumer's Lender of Last Resort." Federal Reserve Bank of Kansas City *Economic Review* (March/April 1990): 5–17.

Catanach, Wallace M. "Check Collections." Thesis. Graduate School of Banking of the American Institute of Banking. New Brunswick, NJ. June 1939.

Cohen, Lizabeth. *Making a New Deal: Industrial Workers in Chicago, 1919–1939.* (Cambridge, MA: Cambridge University Press, 1990).

Consumer Bankers Association. "Check-cashing Services Study." Monograph of study. Roper Organization Inc. December 1989.

Consumer Federation of America. "National Survey of Check Cashing Outlets." Unpublished report. September 1987.

———. "Bank Fees on Consumer Accounts: The Fifth Annual National Survey." Unpublished report. June 1988.

———. "Check-cashing Outlet Fees: Still High and Climbing." Unpublished report. December 1989.

———. "Ten Years after Financial Deregulation: The Sixth Annual National Bank Fee Survey." Unpublished report. June 1990.

Danziger, Sheldon, and Peter Gottschalk. *Uneven Tides: Rising Inequality in America.* (New York: Russell Sage Foundation, 1993).

De Roover, Raymond. "The Three Golden Balls of the Pawnbrokers." *Bulletin of the Business Historical Society* 20 (1946): 117–124.

Dornberg, John. "Vienna's Dorotheum: A Singular Auction House and Hockshop." *Smithsonian* 21 (December 1990): 110–120.

Economic Report of the President. (Washington, DC: U.S. Government Printing Office, 1991).

Ernst & Young. "An Economic Study of the Performance and Viability of the Licensed New York Check Cashing Industry." Report prepared for the Check Cashers' Association of New York. June 1992.

Federal Financial Institutions Examination Council. "A Citizen's Guide to the CRA." June 1992.

Fletcher, P. Taylor. *Business Under the Balls.* (Azusa, CA: Fletcher P. Taylor, 1992).

Foulke, Roy. *The Sinews of American Commerce.* (New York: Dun & Bradstreet, 1941).

Gagerman, Jerome S. "Professional Check Cashers and the Compliance Implications of the Money Laundering Control Act." Manuscript, August 1, 1990.

Glenn, John M., et al. *Russell Sage Foundation 1907–1946.* (New York: Russell Sage Foundation, 1947).

Goodhart, C. A. E. *Money, Information and Uncertainty.* (Cambridge, MA: MIT Press, 1989).

Green, Timothy. "From a Pawnshop to Patron of the Arts in Five Centuries." *Smithsonian* 22 (July 1991): 59–69.

Greenhut, Melvin L., et al. *The Economics of Imperfect Competition: A Spacial Approach.* (Cambridge, England: Cambridge University Press, 1987).

Greenspan, Alan. Speech at The Annual Conference on Bank Structure and Competition held at the Federal Reserve Bank of Chicago. May 10, 1990.

Gregory, Charles, and Frank Norton. *Open and Operate Your Own Pawnshop.* (Duluth, MN: StarNorth Publications, 1985).

Gross, Laura. "Branch Cuts Seen Hurting Minorities." *American Banker* (February 23, 1987).

Hammond, Bray. *Banks and Politics in America: From the Revolution to the Civil War.* (Princeton, NJ: Princeton University Press, 1957).

Hardaker, Alfred. *A Brief History of Pawnbroking.* (London: Jackson, Ruston, and Keeson, 1892).

Hill, Forest Garnett. "Pawnbroking." In *Encyclopedia Britannica.* (Chicago: William Benton, 1968).

Hudson, Kenneth. *Pawnbroking, An Aspect of British Social History.* (London: Bodley Head, 1982).

Humphrey, David B., and Allen N. Berger. "Market Failure and Resource Use: Economic Incentives to Use Different Payment Instruments." In Humphrey, David B. (ed.). *The U.S. Payment System: Efficiency, Risk and the Role of the Federal Reserve.* (Boston, MA: Kluwer Academic, 1990).

Illinois Department of Financial Institutions. *Annual Report.* 1980.

———. *Annual Report.* 1989.

Kemlage, Donald J. "More about Branch Banking and Check-cashing Outlets in New York State." In Reeb, Donald, et al. *Economic Profile of the Check Cashers' Industry.* A Report to the New York State Banking Department. May 1991. Appendix G.

Kemlage, Donald J., and Edward Renshaw. "Branch Bank Closings in Low-income Areas of NYC and Check-cashing Outlets." In Reeb, Donald, et al. *Economic Profile of the Check Cashers' Industry.* A Report to the New York State Banking Department. May 1991. Appendix 7.

Kennickell, Arthur, and Janice Shack-Marquez. "Changes in Family Finances from 1983 to 1989: Evidence from the Survey of Consumer Finances." *Federal Reserve Bulletin.* January 1992.

Kirkman, Patrick. *Electronic Funds Transfer Systems: The Revolution in Cashless Banking and Payment Methods.* (London: Basil Blackwell, 1987).

Kleinfield, N. R. "Running the Little Man's Bank." *New York Times.* August 13, 1989, 37.

Krooss, Herman E., and Martin R. Blyn. *A History of Financial Intermediaries* (New York: Random House, 1971).

Kuznets, Solomon. "Pawnbroking." In Seligman, Edwin R. A. (ed.). *Encyclopaedia of the Social Sciences* (New York: Macmillan, 1933).

Lamberte, Mario. "An Analysis of the Role of Pawnshops in the Financial System." Philippines Institute for Development Studies Working Paper No. 88-04. 1988.

Leichter, Franz. "Banking on the Rich: Commercial Bank Branch Closings and Openings in the New York Metropolitan Area, 1978–88." Manuscript. January 1989.

Levine, Samuel. *A Treatise on the Law of Pawnbroking as Governed by the Principals of Common Law, and as Modified by the Statutes of the Different States of the United States, and the Ordinances of the Municipalities Regulating Pawnbroking.* (New York: Samuel Levine, 1911).

———. *The Business of Pawnbroking: A Guide and a Defense.* (New York: D. Halpern Company, 1913).

Linnen, Beth M. "Repricing Savings Accounts Builds Fee Income." *Savings Institutions* 104 (8) (August 1983): 116–119.

Litan, Robert E. *What Should Banks Do?* (Washington DC: The Brookings Institution, 1987).

Loewenstein, George. "The Fall and Rise of Psychological Explanations in the Economics of Intertemporal Choice." In Loewenstein, George, and Jon Elster (eds.). *Choice Over Time.* (New York: Russell Sage Foundation, 1992). pp. 3–34.

———, and Richard Thaler. "Intertemporal Choice." *Journal of Economic Perspectives* 3 (4) (Fall 1989): 181–193.

Lohr, Steve. "Pawnbrokers in Britain Draw Affluent Clientele." *New York Times.* September 7, 1987. pp. 25–26.

Lueck, Thomas. "Banks Shut in Poor Areas Stir Worries." *New York Times.* August 17, 1988.

Mano, D. Keith. "Pawnbroker's Soliloquy." *National Review* 37 (March 22, 1985): 58–59.

Marec, Yannick. *Le 'Clou' Rouennais: des origines à nos jours (1778–1982) du Mont de piété au Crédit municipal.* (Rouen: Editions du P'tit Normand, 1983).

Mayer, Susan E., and Christopher Jencks. "Poverty and the Distribution of Material Hardship." *Journal of Human Resources* 24 (1) (Winter 1989): 88–114.

Michelman, Irving S. *Consumer Finance: A Case History in American Business.* (New York: Fell, 1966).

Minkes, A. L. "The Decline of Pawnbroking." *Economica* 20 (February 1953): 10–23.

Nathan, Harold C. "Economic Analysis of Usury Laws." *Journal of Bank Research* 10 (Winter 1980): 200–211.

Neifeld, M. R. *Personal Finance Comes of Age.* (New York: Harper & Brothers, 1939).

New Jersey Department of the Public Advocate. "Who's Checking?" January 1988.

Nugent, Rolf. *Consumer Credit and Economic Stability.* (New York: Russell Sage Foundation, 1939).

O'Hara, Maureen, and David Easley. "The Postal Savings System in the Depression." *Journal of Economic History* 39 (3) (September 1979): 741–753.

Patterson, William R. *The Relation of State and Municipality to Pawnbroking in Europe and the United States.* Ph.D. Diss. University of Pennsylvania. 1898.

———. "Pawnbroking in Europe and the United States." U.S. Department of Labor *Bulletin* 4 (1899): 173–310.

Provident Loan Society of New York. *Fifty Years of Remedial Lending.* Fiftieth anniversary commemorative booklet. (New York: Provident Loan Society, 1944).

———. *Annual Report.* Various years.

Raby, Cornelius R. *The Regulation of Pawnbroking.* (New York: Russell Sage Foundation, 1924).

Reeb, Donald, et al. *Economic Profile of the Check Cashers' Industry.* A Report to the New York State Banking Department. May 1991.

Renshaw, Edward. "Regulation of the Dedicated Check-cashing Industry." In Reeb, Donald, et al. *Economic Profile of the Check Cashers' Industry.* A Report to the New York State Banking Department. May 1991.

Richtel, Matt. "Banking on Check Cashing." *The Oakland Tribune.* September 19, 1993.

Robinson, Louis, and Maude E. Stearns. *Ten Thousand Small Loans.* (New York: Russell Sage Foundation, 1930).

Rotella, Elyce. "Visiting Uncle: Pawnshop Activity and the Business Cycle in the Late Nineteenth Century." Unpublished ms. 1989.

Rubin, Edward L. "Putting Deregulation to Work for the Low-income Consumer." *Indiana Law Journal* 67 (1992): 213–249.

Sale, Kirkpatrick. *The Conquest of Paradise: Christopher Columbus and the Columbian Legacy.* (New York: Alfred A. Knopf, 1990).

Schwed, Peter. *God Bless Pawnbrokers.* (New York: Dodd, Mead & Company, 1975).

Shaughnessy, Rick. "Pawnshops: Lenders of Last Resort." *The San Diego Union Tribune.* November 29, 1993. pp. C-1–C-2.

Sherraden, Michael. *Assets and the Poor: A New American Welfare Policy.* (Armonk, NY: M. E. Sharpe, 1991).

Simpson, William R., et al. *Hockshop.* (New York: Random House, 1954).

Skidmore, David. "Chicago Bank is Denied Acquisition over Redlining Law." *The Philadelphia Inquirer.* February 17, 1989. p. 15-C.

Skully, Michael T. "Lending Collateral Problems and the Pawnbroker Solution: The Development of the Pawnshop Industry in Asia." Unpublished ms. November 1992.

Steinberg, Stephen. *The Ethnic Myth: Race, Ethnicity, and Class in America*. (Boston: Beacon Press, 1981).

Stix, Margaret, Errol Louis, and Susan Reynolds. "The New Redlining: A Study of Branch Closings in New York City 1977–84." (New York: Community Training and Resource Center, 1986).

Swagler, Roger M., and Paula Wheeler. "Rental-Purchase Agreements: A Preliminary Investigation of Consumer Attitudes and Behaviors." *The Journal of Consumer Affairs* (Summer 1989): 145–160.

Tebbutt, Melanie. *Making Ends Meet: Pawnbroking and Working-Class Credit*. (New York: St. Martin's Press, 1983).

United States Bureau of the Census. *Historical Statistics of the United States, Colonial Times to 1970*. (Washington, DC: U.S. Government Printing Office, 1975).

United States General Accounting Office. *Banking Services: Changes in Fees and Deposit Account Interest Rates Since Deregulation*. (Washington, DC: U.S. Government Printing Office, 1987).

———. *Government Check Cashing Issues*. (Washington, DC: U.S. Government Printing Office, 1988).

Wayne, Leslie. "New Hopes in Inner Cities: Banks Offering Mortgages." *New York Times*. March 14, 1992.

Whelan, T. S. *The Pawnshop in China*. (Ann Arbor: Center for Chinese Studies, the University of Michigan, 1979).

Wolf, Irving J. "The Licensed Check-cashing Industry in New York City." MBA Thesis. Pace University. September 1975.

Zamba, Michael J. "Closed Banks Worry Neighbors." *Christian Science Monitor*. May 8, 1987.

Index

Boldface numbers refer to figures and tables.

Texas, 36, 45, 46, 47, 53, 56n, 63, 121
three ball symbol, 14–15, 15n
transaction costs: of CCOs, 113–114, 125, 143; of pawnbrokers, 112–113, 143
transportation costs, 17, 17n, 49–50; and fees, 114, 118
trust issue, 116–118, 117n

U

"uncle," origin of term, 18–19
unemployment, 6, 69, 102, 148
Uniform Small Loan Laws, 32
unions, 34–35
unit banking laws, 33
United Kingdom, 34n
unregulated market rates: on check-cashing, 59, 64; on pawnshop loans, 39
urban areas, 2; and bank branches, 90; and CCOs, 62–64; and pawnshops, 16–17, 18, 47; and safety, 30

usury laws, 20, 42; effect of, on consumers, 31–32, 119–120; and pawnshops, 49–50, 52n, 116, 139–140
utility bill payments, 54

V

Vanderbilt, Cornelius, 24

W

Wall Street Journal, 80
Washington, D.C., 41, 92, 95, **95**
Washington state, 57
welfare (AFDC) checks, 30, 56, 77, 77n; distributed by CCOs, 126
Western Union Company, 3–4, 65
Wheeler, P., 80
whites, 75, 101
Wilmington, Delaware, 44
wire transfers, 4, 54, 55, 56, 57, 65
Wisconsin, 47, 54n, 57n
Wolf, I., 33, 34, 56n